LEARNINGEXPRESS

THE BASICS MADE EASY . . .
IN 20 MINUTES A DAY!

A New Approach to "Mastering The Basics." An innovative 20-step self-study program helps you learn at your own pace and make visible progress in just 20 minutes a day.

GRAMMAR ESSENTIALS
HOW TO STUDY
IMPROVE YOUR WRITING FOR WORK
MATH ESSENTIALS
PRACTICAL SPELLING
PRACTICAL VOCABULARY
READ BETTER, REMEMBER MORE
THE SECRETS OF TAKING ANY TEST

Become a Better Student–*Quickly*
Become a More Marketable Employee–*Fast*
Get a Better Job–*Now*

READ BETTER, REMEMBER MORE

Second Edition

Elizabeth Chesla

NEW YORK

Library of Congress Cataloging-in-Publication Data

Chesla, Elizabeth L.
Read better, remember more / Elizabeth Chesla. — 2nd ed.
     p.   cm.
    Rev. ed. of: How to read and remember more in 20 minutes a day. 1st ed. ©1997.
    ISBN 1-57685-336-5 (pbk.)
    1. Reading comprehension 2. Reading (Adult education)
I. Chesla, Elizabeth L. How to read and remember more in 20 minutes a day   II. Title.
LB1050.45.C443 2000
428.4'3—dc21

                                  00-058787

Printed in the United States of America
9 8 7 6 5 4 3 2 1
Second Edition

For Further Information
For information on LearningExpress, other LearningExpress products, or bulk sales,
please call or write to us at:
    LearningExpress®
    900 Broadway
    Suite 604
    New York, NY 10003

Visit LearningExpress on the World Wide Web at www.LearnX.com

CONTENTS

INTRODUCTION
HOW TO USE THIS BOOK

The 20 practical chapters in this book are designed to help you better understand and remember what you read. Because you need to *understand* what you read in order to remember it, many chapters focus on reading comprehension strategies that will help you improve your overall reading ability and effectiveness.

Each chapter focuses on a specific reading skill so that you can build your reading skills step by step in just 20 minutes a day. Practice exercises in each chapter allow you to put the reading strategies you learn into immediate practice. If you read a chapter a day, Monday through Friday, and do all the exercises carefully, you should be able to understand—and remember—much more of what you read by the end of one month of study.

The 20 chapters are divided into four sections. Each section focuses on a related set of reading skills:

Section One:	Setting Yourself Up for Reading Success
Section Two:	Getting—and Remembering—the Gist of It
Section Three:	Improving Your Reading IQ
Section Four:	Reader, Detective, Writer

Each section begins with a brief explanation of that section's focus and ends with a chapter that reviews the main ideas of that section. The practice exercises allow you to combine all of the reading strategies you learned in that section.

Although each chapter is an effective skill builder on its own, it's important that you proceed through this book in order, from Chapter 1 through Chapter 20. Each chapter builds on the skills and ideas discussed in previous chapters. If you don't have a thorough understanding of the concepts in Chapter 4, for example, you may have difficulty with the concepts in Chapters 5-20. The reading and practice passages will also increase in length and complexity with each chapter. Be sure you thoroughly understand each chapter before moving on to the next one.

Each chapter provides several practical exercises that ask you to use the strategies you've just learned. To help you be sure you're on the right track, each chapter also provides answers and explanations for the practice questions. Each chapter also includes practical "skill building" suggestions for how to continue practicing these skills throughout the rest of the day, the week, and beyond.

GET "IN THE MOOD" FOR READING

Your success as a reader, much like the success of an athlete, depends not only on your skills but also upon your state of mind. This book will help you improve your skills, but *you* need to provide the proper atmosphere and attitude.

CREATE AN ATMOSPHERE THAT INVITES SUCCESS

There are many reasons why people may have difficulty understanding or remembering what they read. Sometimes they're too busy thinking about other things. Sometimes they haven't gotten enough sleep. Sometimes the vocabulary is too difficult. And sometimes they're simply not interested in the subject matter.

Perhaps you've experienced one or more of these difficulties. Sometimes these factors are beyond your control, but many times you can help ensure success in your reading task by making sure that you read at the right time and in the right place. Though reading seems like a passive act, it is a task that requires energy and concentration. You'll understand and remember more if you read when you have sufficient energy and in an environment that helps you concentrate.

Therefore, determine **when** you are most alert. Do you concentrate best in the early morning? At lunch time? Late in the afternoon? In the evening? Find your optimum concentration time.

Then, determine **where** you're able to concentrate best. What kind of environment do you need for maximum attention to your task? Consider everything in that environment: how it looks, feels, and sounds. Do you need to be in a comfortable, warm place, or does that kind of environment put you to sleep? Do you need to be in a brightly lit room? Or does softer lighting help you focus? Do you prefer a desk or a table? Or would you rather curl up on a couch? Are you the kind of person that likes some background noise—a TV, radio, the buzz of people eating in a restaurant? If you like music, what kind of music is best for your concentration? Or do you need absolute silence?

If you're preoccupied with other tasks or concerns and the reading can wait, let it wait. If you're distracted by more pressing concerns, chances are you'll end up reading the same paragraphs over and over without really understanding or remembering what you've read. Instead, see if there's something you can do to address those concerns. Then, when you're more relaxed, come back to your reading task. If it's not possible to wait, do your best to keep your attention on your reading. Keep reminding yourself that it has to get done, and that there's little you can do about your other concerns at the moment.

You may also want to plan a small reward for yourself when you finish your reading task. This will give you something to look forward to and give you positive reinforcement for a job well done.

CREATE AN ATTITUDE THAT INVITES SUCCESS

In addition to creating the right atmosphere, you need to approach reading with the right *attitude*. The "right" attitude is a positive one. If you have something to read and you tell yourself, "I'll never understand this," chances are you won't. You've just conditioned yourself to fail. Instead, condition yourself for success. Tell yourself that no matter how difficult the reading task, you'll learn something from it. You'll become a better reader. You can understand, and you can remember.

Have a positive attitude about the reading material, too. If you tell yourself, "This is going to be boring," you also undermine your chances for reading success. Even if you're not interested in the topic you must read about, remember that you're reading it for a reason; you have something to gain. Keep your goal clearly in mind. Again, plan to reward yourself in some way when you've completed your reading task. (And remember that the knowledge you gain from reading is its own reward.)

If you get frustrated, keep in mind that the right atmosphere and attitude can make all the difference in how much you benefit from this book.

Happy reading.

READ BETTER, REMEMBER MORE

Second Edition

PRE-TEST

Before you begin this book, you might want to get an idea of how much you already know and how much you need to learn. If so, take the following pretest.

The pretest consists of two parts. Part I contains 10 multiple-choice questions addressing some of the key concepts covered in this book. In Part II, you'll read two passages and answer questions about the ideas and strategies used in those passages.

Even if you earn a perfect score on the pretest, you will undoubtedly benefit from working through the chapters in this book, since only a fraction of the information in these chapters is covered on the pretest. On the other hand, if you miss a lot of questions on the pretest, don't despair. These chapters are designed to teach you reading comprehension and retention skills step by step. You may find that the chapters take you a little more than 20 minutes to complete, but that's okay. Take your time and enjoy the learning process.

You can record your answers on a separate sheet of paper, or, if you own this book, you can simply circle the answers below.

Take as much time as you need for the pretest, though you shouldn't need much longer than half an hour. When you finish, check your answers against the answer key provided at the end of the pretest. The answer key shows you which chapters correspond to each question.

NOTE: Do not use a dictionary for this pretest.

PART I

1. When you read, it's important to have:
    a. complete silence
    b. a dictionary
    c. a pen or pencil
    d. (b) and (c)
    e. (a) and (c)

2. Most texts use which underlying organizational structure?
    a. cause and effect
    b. order of importance
    c. assertion and support
    d. comparison and contrast

3. The main idea of a paragraph is often stated in:
    a. a topic sentence
    b. a transitional phrase
    c. the middle of the paragraph
    d. the title

4. Which of the following sentences expresses an opinion?
    a. Many schools practice bilingual education.
    b. Bilingual education hurts students more than it helps them.
    c. Bilingual classes are designed to help immigrant students.
    d. Bilingual classes are taught in a language other than English.

5. A summary should include:
    a. the main idea only
    b. the main idea and major supporting ideas
    c. the main idea, major supporting ideas, and minor supporting details
    d. minor supporting details only

6. Before you read, you should:
   a. Do nothing. Just jump right in and start reading.
   b. Stretch your arms and legs.
   c. Read the introduction and section headings.
   d. Look up information about the author.

7. Words and phrases like "for example" and "likewise" show readers:
   a. the relationship between ideas
   b. the main idea of the paragraph
   c. the organization of the text
   d. the author's opinion

8. *Tone* is:
   a. the way a word is pronounced
   b. the techniques a writer uses to persuade readers
   c. the meaning of a word or phrase
   d. the mood or attitude conveyed by words

9. When you take notes, you should include:
   a. definitions of key terms
   b. your questions and reactions
   c. major supporting ideas
   d. (a) and (c) only
   e. (a), (b), and (c)

10. When you read, you should:
    a. never write on the text
    b. underline key ideas
    c. highlight every fact
    d. skip over unfamiliar words

PART II

Read the following passages carefully and answer the questions that follow.

Passage 1

Being a secretary is a lot like being a parent. After a while, your boss becomes dependent upon you, just as a child is dependent upon his or her parents. Like a child who must ask permission before going out, you'll find your boss coming to you for permission, too. "Can I have a meeting on Tuesday at 3:30?" you might be asked, because you're the one who keeps track of your boss's schedule. You will also find yourself cleaning up after your boss a lot, tidying up papers and files the same way a parent tucks away a child's toys and clothes. And, like a parent protects his or her children from outside dangers, you will find yourself protecting your boss from certain "dangers"—unwanted callers, angry clients, and upset subordinates.

11. The main idea of this passage is:
    a. Secretaries are treated like children.
    b. Bosses treat their secretaries like children.
    c. Secretaries and parents have similar roles.
    d. Bosses depend too much upon their secretaries.

12. Which of the following is the topic sentence of the paragraph?
    a. Being a secretary is a lot like being a parent.
    b. After a while, your boss becomes dependent upon you, just as a child is dependent upon his or her parents.
    c. You will also find yourself cleaning up after your boss a lot, tidying up papers and files the same way a parent tucks away a child's toys and clothes.
    d. None of the above.

13. According to the passage, secretaries are like parents in which of the following ways?
    a. They make their boss's life possible.
    b. They keep their bosses from things that might harm or bother them.
    c. They're always cleaning and scrubbing things.
    d. They don't get enough respect.

14. This passage uses which point of view?
    a. first person
    b. second person
    c. third person
    d. first and second person

15. The tone of this passage suggests that:
    a. The writer is angry about how secretaries are treated.
    b. The writer thinks secretaries do too much work.
    c. The writer is slightly amused by how similar the roles of secretaries and parents are.
    d. The writer is both a secretary and a parent.

16. The sentence "=t'Can I have a meeting on Tuesday at 3:30?' you might be asked, because you're the one who keeps track of your boss's schedule" is a:
    a. main idea
    b. major supporting idea
    c. minor supporting idea
    d. transition

17. "Being a secretary is a lot like being a parent" is:
    a. a fact
    b. an opinion
    c. neither
    d. both

18. The word "subordinates" probably means:
    a. employees
    b. parents
    c. clients
    d. secretaries

Passage 2

Over 150 years ago, in the middle of the nineteenth century, the Austrian Monk Gregor Mendel provided us with the first scientific explanation for why children look like their parents. By experimenting with different strains of peas in his garden, he happened to discover the laws of heredity.

Mendel bred tall pea plants with short pea plants, expecting to get medium-height pea plants in his garden. However, mixing tall and short "parent" plants did not produce medium-sized "children" as a result. Instead, it produced some generations that were tall and others that were short.

This led Mendel to hypothesize that all traits (such as eye color or height) have both dominant or recessive characteristics. If the dominant characteristic is present, it *suppresses* the recessive characteristic. For example, tallness (T) might be dominant and shortness (t) recessive. Where there is a dominant T, offspring will be tall. Where there is no dominant T, offspring will be short.

Imagine, for example, that each parent has two "markers" for height: TT, Tt, or tt. The child inherits one marker from each parent.

If both parents have full tallness (TT and TT), the child will definitely be tall; any marker the child could receive is the dominant marker for tallness. If both parents have full shortness (tt and tt), then the child will likewise be short; there are no dominant Ts to suppress the shortness. However, if both parents have a mix of markers (Tt and Tt), then there are four possible combinations: TT, Tt, tT, and tt. Of course, TT will result in a tall child and tt in a short child. If the child receives one T and one t, the child will also be tall, since tallness is dominant and will suppress the marker for shortness. Thus, if both parents have a mix (Tt and Tt), the child has a 75% chance of being tall and a 25% chance of being short.

This is an oversimplification, but it is the basis of Mendel's theory, which was later proven by the discovery of genes and DNA. We now know that characteristics such as height are determined by several genes, not just one pair. Still, Mendel's contribution to the world of science is immeasurable.

19. The main idea of this passage is that:
    a. Mendel was a great scientist.
    b. Children inherit height from their parents.
    c. Mendel discovered the laws of heredity.
    d. Pea plants show how human heredity works.
20. Two key terms explained in this passage are:
    a. "Gregor Mendel" and "pea plants"
    b. "dominant characteristics" and "laws of heredity"
    c. "recessive characteristics" and "tallness"
    d. "genes" and "DNA"
21. In his first experiments with pea plants, Mendel:
    a. got medium pea plants, as he expected
    b. got medium pea plants, which he didn't expect
    c. got short and tall pea plants, as he expected
    d. got short and tall pea plants, which he didn't expect
22. To "suppress" means:
    a. to hold back or block out
    b. to destroy
    c. to change or transform
    d. to bring out

23. The phrase "happened to discover" in the first paragraph suggests that:

   a. Mendel wasn't careful in his experiments.

   b. Mendel didn't set out to discover the laws of heredity.

   c. Mendel was lucky he discovered anything at all.

   d. Mendel could have discovered much more if he'd tried.

24. Which of the following sentences best summarizes the first paragraph?

   a. Mendel's experiments with pea plants led him to discover the laws of heredity.

   b. Mendel's experiments with pea plants produced unexpected results.

   c. Mendel was both a monk and a scientist.

   d. Mendel's discovery was an accident.

25. According to the passage:

   a. there are two genes for tallness

   b. tallness is a recessive trait

   c. dominant traits suppress recessive ones

   d. children have a 75% chance of being tall

26. According to the passage, a child who has the "Tt" combination has which parents?

   a. TT and TT

   b. TT and tt

   c. tt and tt

   d. Tt and Tt

27. The passage suggests that:

   a. the laws of heredity are still unproven

   b. the laws of heredity are much more complicated than the example indicates

   c. Mendel deserves more credit than he gets

   d. parents should seek genetic counseling

28. This passage is organized according to which organizational strategy?

   a. cause and effect

   b. chronology

   c. general to specific

   d. order of importance

29. The sentence "Still, Mendel's contribution to the world of science is immeasurable" is a:

   a. fact

   b. opinion

   c. neither

   d. both

30. The tone of this passage is best described as:

   a. informative

   b. critical

   c. authoritative

   d. indifferent

ANSWER KEY

Question	Answer	Chapter
1.	d	Intro, 1
2.	c	11
3.	a	6
4.	b	12
5.	b	8, 19
6.	c	1
7.	a	11
8.	d	17
9.	e	9
10.	b	Intro, 4, 8, 9
11.	c	6
12.	a	6
13.	b	2
14.	b	16
15.	c	17
16.	c	7
17.	b	12
18.	a	4
19.	c	6
20.	b	9, 10
21.	d	2
22.	a	4
23.	b	16, 18
24.	a	8, 19
25.	c	2
26.	d	2
27.	b	2
28.	c	11
29.	b	12
30.	a	17

SECTION 1

SETTING YOURSELF UP FOR READING SUCCESS

Even the most experienced readers had to start somewhere, and that somewhere is a place they keep coming back to: the basics.

The chapters in this section will arm you with basic reading comprehension strategies. You'll learn a few key strategies that will help you better understand, and therefore better remember, what you read. In this section, you'll learn how to:

- Use pre-reading strategies
- Use a dictionary
- Find the basic facts in a passage
- Determine the meaning of unfamiliar words in context

These are fundamental skills that will give you a solid foundation for reading success. Strategies to help you remember what you read are also included in each chapter.

CHAPTER | 1

Reading success depends upon your active participation as a reader. This chapter will show you how to use pre-reading strategies to "warm up" to any reading task.

PRE-READING STRATEGIES

The difference between a good reader and a frustrated reader is much like the difference between an athlete and a sports fan: the athlete actively participates in the sport while the fan remains on the sidelines. A good reader is always actively engaged in the reading task. Frustrated readers, on the other hand, think of reading as a passive "sideline" task, something that doesn't require their active participation. As a result, they often have difficulty understanding and remembering what they read.

Perhaps the most important—and most basic—thing you can do to improve your reading skills is to get off the sidelines and *become an active reader.* This doesn't mean you should work up a sweat while reading, but it does mean that you should be actively involved with the text whenever you read.

Be an Active Reader
You'll understand and remember more if you become an active reader.

To become an active reader, it helps to think of reading as a dialogue where you talk with the writer, not a one-way conversation where you just sit back and let the writer talk at you. When you talk with people, you nod, talk back, and ask questions. You watch the facial expressions and gestures of the speakers and listen to their tone of voice to help you understand what they're saying. Active readers apply these same strategies to reading. The chapters in this book will show you exactly how to do that.

In this chapter, you will learn effective pre-reading strategies that you can use to prepare for reading tasks. Just as athletes enhance their performance by stretching before they go out on the court or field, active readers can significantly increase how much they understand and remember if they take a few minutes to "stretch" before they read.

Here are three pre-reading strategies that will dramatically improve your chances of reading success:

1. breaking up the reading task
2. reading the pre-text
3. skimming ahead and jumping back

BREAK IT UP INTO MANAGEABLE TASKS

The first step you can take as an active reader is to plan a strategy for your reading task. Readers sometimes get frustrated because the reading task before them seems impossible. "A hundred pages!" they might say. "How am I going to get through this? How am I going to *remember* all this?"

Building a skyscraper or renovating a house may seem like an impossible task at first, too. But these things get accomplished by breaking the whole into manageable parts. Buildings get put up one floor and one brick at a time; houses get renovated one room and one section at a time. And reading gets done in the same way: little by little, piece by piece, page by page.

Thus, one of your first strategies should be to break up your reading into manageable tasks. If you have to read a chapter that's 40 pages long, can you divide those 40 pages into four sections of 10 pages each? Or is the chapter already divided into sections that you can use as starting and stopping points?

In general, if the text you're reading is only a few pages (say, less than five), you probably don't need to break up the task into different reading sessions. But if it's more than five pages, you'll probably benefit from breaking it into two halves. If you find the first half goes really well, go ahead—jump right into the second. But you'll feel more confident knowing that you can take it one section at a time.

The Benefits of Starting and Stopping

By breaking up a text into manageable tasks, you do more than just reduce frustration. You also improve the chances that you'll remember more. That's because your brain can only absorb so much information in a certain amount of time. Especially if the text is filled with facts or ideas that are new to you, you need to give yourself time to absorb that information. Breaking the reading into manageable tasks gives you a chance to digest the information in each section.

In addition, simply because of the way the human mind works, people tend to remember most what comes first and what comes last. Think about the last movie you saw, for example. If you're like most people, you can probably remember exactly how it began and exactly how it ended. You know what happened in the middle, of course, but those details aren't as clear as the details of the beginning and the end. This is just the nature of the learning process. Thus, if you break up a reading task into several sections, there are more starting and stopping points—more beginnings and endings to remember. There will be less material in the middle to be forgotten.

Scheduling Breaks

Part of breaking up a reading task means scheduling in breaks. If you've divided 40 pages into four sections of ten pages each, be sure to give yourself a brief pause between each section. Otherwise, you lose the benefits you'd get from starting and stopping. Perhaps you can read ten pages, take a five minute stretch, and then read ten more. You might do the same for the other 20 pages tomorrow.

Use Existing Section Breaks

Writers will often help you learn and remember information by dividing the text into manageable chunks for you. Page through this book, for example, to see how it breaks up information for you. Notice that the book is divided into sections; the sections are divided into chapters. The chapters are then divided into summaries, main strategies (indicated by the headings, or subtitles), practice exercises, answers, a review, and skill building strategies. All you need to do is decide how many chunks you'll read at a time.

PRACTICE 1

Keeping in mind your optimum concentration time, develop a strategy for reading this book. Will you do one chapter each day? Complete each chapter in one sitting? Will you read the chapter in the morning and do the exercises in the evening? Write your strategy on a separate piece of paper and keep it in the front of this book.

Answer

Answers will vary, depending upon your preferences and personality. Here's one possible reading plan:

- Read one chapter each day, Monday through Friday.
- Reading time: 8:00–8:30, right after breakfast. (I can't concentrate on an empty stomach.)
- Reading place: At the kitchen table. I can spread my books and papers out, the light is bright, and it's usually quiet.
- Music: I'll turn on the classical radio station—the public station that doesn't have commercials (which really distract me). The soft music will help me relax and drown out the hum of traffic.
- Other: I must put the newspaper aside until after I finish my chapter. I'll save reading the paper as a "reward."

READ THE PRE-TEXT

Writers generally provide you with a great deal of information before they even begin their main text—and this information will often help you better understand the reading ahead. For example, look at this book. Its cover provides you with a title and lists some of the features of the book.

Inside, on the first few pages, you get the author's name and some information about the publisher. Then comes the table of contents and general introduction and guidelines for how to use this book. Each section has its own introduction, and each chapter begins with a short summary.

Each of these features fall into a category called **pre-text**. Information in the pre-text is designed to help you better understand and remember what you read. It tells you, in advance, the main idea and the purpose of what's ahead. Most texts provide you with one or more of these pre-text features:

- Title
- Subtitle
- Biographical information about the author
- Table of contents
- Introduction or preface
- Section summary

Each pre-text feature tells you information about the writer's purpose and the main ideas that the writer wants to convey. By looking at these reading aids before you begin, you'll get a clear sense of what you're supposed to learn and why. Pre-text features are designed to arouse your interest, raise your expectations, and make information manageable. They introduce you to the key ideas of the text and indicate the major divisions of the text. Reading them will better prepare you to understand and remember what's to come.

Athletes who know the purpose of a practice drill will be more motivated and better prepared to do the exercise well. Likewise, you'll be more motivated and better prepared to read a text if you're aware of its purpose and what you're about to learn.

PRACTICE 2

If you haven't read the pre-text of this book, please STOP working through this chapter and read the pre-text now. In particular, read through the Table of Contents and Introduction as well as the summary of Section 1. Then, answer the following questions:

1. Why should you do the chapters in order?
2. What is included at the end of each section?

3. What two things should you do to improve your chances of reading success?

4. What are the chapters in Section 1 about?

Answer

If you're at all uncertain about the correct answers to this practice exercise, re-read the pre-text. When you find the sentences that have the answers, underline them.

SKIM AHEAD AND JUMP BACK

Another important pre-reading strategy is skimming ahead and jumping back. Before you read a section of text, read the summary (if available), and then *skim ahead*. Go through and look at the headings or divisions of the section. How is it broken down? What are the main topics in that section, and in what order are they covered? If the text isn't divided, read the first few words of each paragraph or random paragraphs. What are these paragraphs about? Finally, what key words or phrases are highlighted, underlined, boxed, or bulleted in the text?

Like reading the pre-text, skimming ahead helps prepare you to receive the information to come. You may not realize it, but subconsciously, your mind picks up a lot. When you skim ahead, the key words and ideas you come across will register in your brain. Then, when you read the information more carefully, there's already a "place" for that information to go.

To further strengthen your understanding and memory of what you read, when you finish a chapter or a section, *jump back* and review the text. In this book, you are provided with a review at the end of each chapter called "In Short," but you should also go back and review the highlights of each section when you've finished. Look back at the headings, the information in bullets, and any information that's boxed or otherwise highlighted to show that it's important.

You can jump back at any time in the reading process, and you *should* do it any time you feel that the information is starting to overload. This will help you remember where you've been and where you're going. Skimming ahead and jumping back can also remind you how what you're reading now fits into the bigger picture. This also helps you better understand and remember what you read by allowing you to make connections and place that information in context. When facts and ideas are related to other facts and ideas, you're far more likely to remember them.

In addition, repetition is the key to mastery. So the more you *pre*-view (skim ahead) and *re*view (jump back) information, the more you seal key words and ideas in your memory. Each time you skim ahead and jump back, you strengthen your ability to remember that material.

PRACTICE 3

Skim ahead to Chapter 2, even though you probably aren't going to read the chapter until tomorrow. Skimming ahead doesn't have to happen immediately before you take on the reading task. By skimming ahead now, you can still prepare your mind to receive the ideas to come. Using the headings and other reading aids, list the three main topics covered in Chapter 2.

Read Aloud

If your attention starts to fade while you're reading or the material gets difficult to handle, try reading aloud. If you can *hear* the words as well as *see* them, chances are you'll pay more attention. After all, both your eyes *and* your ears will be at work.

Answers

Asking Questions

Find the Facts

Remember the Facts

IN SHORT

Pre-reading strategies will help you better manage, comprehend, and remember what you read. These strategies include:

- Breaking the text into manageable tasks
- Reading the pre-text
- Skimming ahead and jumping back

In addition, if your attention begins to fade, try reading aloud to engage your ears as well as your eyes.

Skill Building Until Next Time

1. Apply these active reading strategies to everything you read this week.
2. Notice how you prepare for other tasks throughout your day. For example, what do you do to get ready to cook a meal? How might your pre-cooking strategies match up with pre-reading strategies? How much more difficult would something like cooking be if you didn't take those preparatory steps?

CHAPTER | 2

You'll often be expected to remember specific facts and ideas from the text you read. Asking the right questions can help you find and remember that information.

GETTING THE FACTS

Much of what you read today, especially in this "information age," is designed to provide you with information. At work, for example, you might read about a new office procedure or how to use a new computer program. At home, you might read the paper to get the latest news or read about current issues in a magazine. It is therefore very important that you be able to understand the facts and information conveyed in these texts. What will you be expected to remember and know? What do you *want* to remember and know? Asking a series of *who, what, when, where, why,* and *how* questions will help you get these facts so that you can remember them.

ASKING QUESTIONS

The Questions to Ask
Ask the questions *who, what, when, where, why,* and *how* as you read.

In any text you read, certain things happen, and they happen for a reason. To find out why they happened, and, more importantly, why it matters, you need to first establish the facts. Like a detective entering the scene of a crime, you need to answer some basic questions:

- *What* happened (or will happen)?
- *Who* (or *what*) was involved (or will be involved)?
- *When* did it happen (or will happen)?
- *Where?*
- *Why?*
- *How?*

Once you establish the facts, then you can go on to answer the most difficult question: What does it all add up to? What is the writer trying to show or prove? You'll learn more about how to answer this question in Chapter 6.

FIND THE FACTS

To find the facts in a text, you need to be clear about just what a "fact" is. Here's the definition of "fact":

- Something *known* for certain to have happened
- Something *known* for certain to be true
- Something *known* for certain to exist

When you read, the easiest fact to establish is often the action: *what* happened, will happen, or is happening. This is especially true when you come across a difficult sentence. The next step is to determine *who* performed that action. Then, you can find the details: *when, where, why,* and *how.* However, not all of these questions will be applicable in every case.

Let's begin by finding facts in a couple of sentences and then work up to a series of paragraphs. Read the next sentence carefully.

After you complete form 10A, have it signed by a witness or else it will not be considered valid.

Here are four questions you can ask to get the facts from this sentence:

1. What should happen?
2. Who should do it?
3. When?
4. Why?

To find the answer to the first question, look for the main **action** of the sentence. Here, there are two actions: *complete* and *have [it] signed*. But because of the word *after*, you know that *complete* isn't the main action of this sentence. What should happen? The form should be signed.

To answer the second question, "Who should do it?" look for the **people** or other possible **agents of action** in the sentence. Here, there are two of them: *you* and *a witness*. The word *by* tells you who should do the signing.

Next, to answer the third question, look for words that indicate **time**—specific dates or adverbs such as *before, after, during*, and so on. Here, the word *after* gives the answer: *after you complete the form*. Finally, the fourth question: Why? Writers will often provide clues with words such as *because, so that*, and *in order to*. Here, the last phrase in the sentence tells you that the form must be signed so it can be considered valid.

By asking and answering these questions, you can pull the facts out of the sentence to help you better understand and remember them. Of course, the questions, and sometimes the order in which you ask them, will vary from sentence to sentence. Learning to ask the right questions comes from practice.

PRACTICE 1

Read the sentence below carefully and answer the questions that follow. It's a long sentence, so take it one question at a time.

In 1998, Pathman Marketing conducted a study that showed people are willing to spend money on products that will improve their quality of life.

1. What happened?
2. Who did it?
3. When?
4. What did it show?

Answers

1. A study was conducted.
2. Pathman Marketing.
3. 1998.
4. People will spend money on products to improve their quality of life.

REMEMBER THE FACTS

Asking *who, what, when, where, why,* and *how* questions makes your reading process more active and enables you to find the facts in any passage. These facts will often be what you'll need to remember. Because you've actively looked for this information, it will be easier for you to remember. In addition, you usually aren't expected to remember or know everything in a paragraph. By pulling out the facts, you reduce the amount of material you'll have to remember.

PRACTICE 2

Now look at a complete paragraph. Read it carefully, and answer the questions that follow. You'll notice there are more questions because there is more information to remember.

> In order to apply for most entry-level positions at the United States Postal Service, you must meet certain minimum requirements. First, you must be at least 18 years of age or older, unless you are 16 or 17 and have already graduated from high school. Second, if you are male, you must be registered with the U.S. Selective Service. Third, you must also be a U.S. citizen or legal resident alien. Fourth, you must be able to lift 70 pounds. Finally, you must have 20/40 vision in one eye and 20/100 vision in the other (glasses are allowed). If you meet these requirements, you can apply when a postal district offers an "application period."

1. *Who* or *what* is this passage about?
2. *How many* requirements are there?
3. *What* are those minimum requirements?
4. *How old* must you be if you have not graduated from high school?
5. *Who* must be registered with the Selective Service?
6. *True or False:* You must have 20/20 vision.
7. *When* can you apply?

Answers

1. This passage is about minimum requirements for working with the United States Postal Service.
2. There are five requirements.
3. You must be 18 if you have not graduated from high school.
   You must be registered with the Selective Service (if male).
   You must be a U.S. citizen or legal resident alien.
   You must be able to lift 70 pounds.
   You must have 20/40 and 20/100 vision.
4. You must be 18 if you have not graduated from high school.
5. Males must be registered with the Selective Service.
6. False. You don't need to have 20/20 vision.
7. You can apply during "application periods."

PRACTICE 3

Now take a look at a passage similar to something you might read in a local newspaper. The passage is divided into several short paragraphs in the style of newspaper articles. Read the passage carefully and then answer the *who, what, when, where, why,* and *how* questions that follow.

According to a recent study conducted by Elmont Community College, distance learning is a legitimate alternative to traditional classroom education.

In February, the college surveyed 1,000 adults across the country to see if distance learning programs measured up to traditional classroom education. Five hundred of those surveyed were enrolled in traditional, on-campus classes and 500 were enrolled in "virtual" classes that "met" online through the Internet. These online classes were offered by

29 different universities. All students surveyed were in degree programs.

A large majority of the distance learning students—87 percent—said they were pleased with their learning experience. "This was a much higher percentage than we expected," said Karen Kaplan, director of the study. In fact, it was just short of the 88 percent of traditional classroom students who claimed they were satisfied.

In addition, many distance learning students reported that the flexibility and convenience of the virtual environment made up for the lack of face-to-face interaction with classmates and instructors. While they missed the human contact, they really needed the ability to attend class any time of the day or night. This is largely due to the fact that nearly all distance learning students—96 percent—hold full-time jobs, compared to only 78 percent of adult students enrolled in traditional classes.

1. What did Elmont Community College do?
2. Why?
3. When?
4. How do distance learning students take classes?
5. How many people were surveyed?
6. What percent of distance learning students were satisfied?
7. Were distance learning students more satisfied, less satisfied, or about the same as regular classroom students?
8. True or false: These were the results that were expected.
9. According to the survey, what makes distance learning a good experience?

Answers

1. Elmont Community College conducted a survey.
2. They conducted the survey to see how distance learning compared to traditional classroom learning.
3. The survey was conducted in February.
4. The distance learning students take classes on-line through the Internet.

5. 1,000 people were surveyed.

6. 87 percent of distance learning students were satisfied.

7. Distance learning students were satisfied about the same (1 percent difference) as regular classroom students.

8. False. These results were not what was expected.

9. Distance learning is a good experience because of the flexibility and convenience of classes on the Internet.

PRACTICE 4

Now it's time for you to write your own *who, what, when, where, why,* and *how* questions. Read the passage below carefully and then ask *who, what, when, where, why,* and *how* questions to find the facts in the passage. Use a separate sheet of paper to list your questions and answers.

Employees who wish to transfer to other divisions or branch offices must fill out a Transfer Request Form. This form can be obtained in the Human Resources Office. The completed form must be signed by the employee and the employee's supervisor. The signed form should then be submitted to Roger Walters in Human Resources. Employees requesting a transfer should receive a response within one month of the date they submit their form.

Answers

Though the facts in the passage remain the same, the exact questions readers ask to find those facts will vary. Here are possible questions along with their answers:

- What should happen? *A Transfer Request Form must be filled out.*
- Who should do it? *Employees who wish to transfer.*
- Where can employees get the form? *Human Resources Office.*
- Who should sign it? *Both the employee and the employee's supervisor.*
- Who should get the completed form? *Roger Walters.*
- When will employees get a response? *Within a month.*

IN SHORT

You'll often have to read and remember texts filled with facts. Ask your-self *who, what, when, where, why,* and *how* questions to find those facts in the texts you read. By pulling out the facts, you call them to your attention, making it easier for you to remember them.

Skill Building Until Next Time

1. As you read the newspaper throughout the week, notice how most articles begin by telling you who, what, when, where, why, and how. This technique gives readers the most important facts right from the start.

2. Answer the who, what, when, where, why, and how questions for other things that you read throughout the week.

CHAPTER | 3

To understand and
remember what you read,
you need to understand
each word in the text.
This chapter will show you
how you can use the
dictionary to improve
your reading skills.

USING THE DICTIONARY

Imagine you are in a New York City subway station waiting for a train when you hear an announcement coming over the loudspeaker:

Ladies and gentlemen, please. . . . the train. . . . doors. . . . next station. . . . express. . . . the approximate . . . please do not. . . . your safety. . . . and give. . . . thank you.

How are you supposed to understand the announcement? It's nearly impossible; you weren't able to hear half of the words in the message.

Similarly, how can you understand what you read if you don't know what some of the words mean?

Many people would understand and remember much more of what they read if they simply had a larger vocabulary. In fact, a limited vocabulary is often what frustrates people more than anything else when it comes to reading. The solution is to work steadily on improving your vocabulary. And the first step is to get in the habit of *looking up any word you come across that you don't know.* Even if you are just going to sit down with the Sunday paper, sit down with a dictionary. Any college edition will do. Don't think of it as work; think of it as an investment in your future. It may be slow going at first, but as you build your vocabulary, you will spend less and less time looking up words. You'll also become increasingly confident as a reader.

Look It Up
When you read, look up every word you don't know.

READ THE ENTIRE DEFINITION

Just about everyone who can read can look up a word in a dictionary. But not everyone knows how to take advantage of all the information a dictionary definition offers. The more you know about a word, the easier it will be to remember what that word means and how it is used.

Readers often cheat themselves by looking only at the first meaning listed in a dictionary definition. There's a lot more to a dictionary entry than that first definition. Many words have more than one possible meaning, and other information provided in the definition can help you better remember the word.

To show you how much a dictionary definition has to offer, let's take the word *leech* as an example. If you were to look it up in a dictionary, you might find the following definition:

> **leech** (lēch) *n.* 1. a small bloodsucking worm usually living in water. 2. a person who drains the resources of another.

Following the word *leech*, is the phonetic spelling of the word—that is, the word is spelled exactly how it sounds. This tells you exactly how to pronounce it. Next, the abbreviation (*n.*) tells you the word's *part of speech*. N stands for *noun*. (You'll see more on this later in the chapter.) Then, you learn that the word has two related but distinct meanings:

- A bloodsucking worm
- A person who drains the resources of another

USE CONTEXT TO PICK THE RIGHT MEANING

Because *leech* has two distinct definitions, you have to decide which definition works best in the *context* of the sentence. The *context* is the words and ideas that surround the word in question. How is the word being used? In what situation? For example, which meaning for *leech* makes the most sense in the context of the following sentences?

> Larry is such a leech. He's always borrowing money and never pays me back.

Clearly, the second meaning of *leech*, "a person who drains the resources of another," makes the most sense in the context of this example. The second definition describes a person; the first definition describes a water-dwelling worm. Notice that if you had closed the dictionary after reading only the first definition, the example above wouldn't make sense.

Here's a sentence in which the first meaning of *leech* would make sense:

> Hundreds of years ago, doctors often used leeches to suck the "bad blood" out of patients.

Leech has two very different definitions. One defines a type of worm, the other a type of person. But you should be able to see that those definitions are actually very closely related. After all, a *person* who is a leech sucks the resources (money, food, material possessions, or whatever) from someone the way a *leech worm* sucks the blood out of a person. Both types of leeches are a drain on whomever they attach themselves to.

PRACTICE 1

Look up the word *slam*. Then, decide which meaning of the word makes the most sense in the context of the following sentence:

The critics *slammed* his new film.

Answer:

Slam has three meanings:

1. to shut forcefully with a loud noise
2. to put or knock or hit forcefully
3. *slang* to criticize severely

The third, slang meaning is clearly the one that makes the most sense in the context of the sentence.

PARTS OF SPEECH

You can distinguish between the two different types of leeches and place them in the proper context. But what if you come across *leech* in a sentence like this?

"Stop *leeching* off of me!" he yelled.

Neither of the previous definitions work in this sentence. That's because in this sentence, *leech* is no longer a noun—the name of a person, place, or thing. It's now a different **part of speech**. And words change their meaning when they change their part of speech.

A word's *part of speech* indicates how that word functions in a sentence. Many words in the English language can function as more than one part of speech. They can be only one part of speech at a time, but they can shift from being a *verb* to a *noun* to an *adjective*, all in the same sentence. Here's an example:

The *dump* truck *dumped* the garbage in the *dump*.

It sounds funny to say "dump" in one sentence three times, but each time the word is used it has a different function—a different part of speech.

There are eight parts of speech, but let's only focus on the four that are most likely to affect meaning: noun, verb, adjective, and adverb. Read the definitions of these parts of speech carefully:

Parts of Speech			
Noun	(n.)	a person, place or thing	(for example, *woman, beach, pencil*)
Verb	(v.)	an action or state of being	(for example, *go, shout, be, feel*)
Adjective	(adj.)	a word that describes a noun	(for example, *red, happy, slow, forty*)
Adverb	(adv.)	a word that describes a verb, adjective, or another adverb	(for example, *happily, slowly, very, quite*)

Parts of speech are important because, as you've already seen, words change their meaning when they change their part of speech. When you look in the dictionary, be sure you're looking up the proper definition. In other words, if a word has different meanings for its different parts of speech, then you need to be sure you're looking at the right part of speech.

PRACTICE 2

Use the definitions of the four parts of speech (noun, verb, adjective, and adverb) to determine the parts of speech of the underlined words below:

1. The <u>dump</u> truck <u>dumped</u> the garbage in the <u>dump</u>.
       a   **b**   **c**

2. Her <u>memory</u> <u>faded</u> <u>slowly</u> as she neared 100.
         a   **b**   **c**

Answers

1. **a.** Here, *dump* is used as an adjective. It describes the truck, which is a noun. It answers the question "What kind of truck?"
   b. Here, *dumped* is a verb. It shows the action that the truck performed.
   c. Here, *dump* is a noun. It's the place where the truck dumped the garbage.

2. a. *Memory* is a noun (a thing).

 b. *Faded* is a verb—the action that her memory performed.

 c. *Slowly* is an adverb. It describes the verb, telling *how* her memory faded.

When Suffixes Change Part of Speech

Words often change parts of speech by adding a **suffix:** two to four letters like -*ness* or -*tion* or -*ify*. *Suffixes* are endings added on to words to change their meanings and make new words. Most adverbs, for example, are formed by adding *ly* to an adjective. Sometimes words with suffixes are not listed in the dictionary. (This often depends on the type of dictionary you're using.) If you can't find a word in the dictionary, it could be because the word has a suffix on it. Try to find another version of that word and see if your word is mentioned in that definition.

When words with suffixes added to them don't have their own listing, they are usually mentioned in the definition for the word from which they're formed. For example, notice how the definition for the word *indecisive* lists two related words formed by suffixes:

> *indecisive* (in-di-sī-siv) *(adj.). not decisive. indecisively* (adv.), *indecisiveness* (n.).

Indecisively and indecisiveness won't have their own dictionary entries because their meanings are so closely related to the meaning of the original word. In this case, you can usually just alter the original definition for the new part of speech. For instance, you might have to change the definition from a verb to a noun—from an action to a thing.

Suffixes that Change Part of Speech

Some suffixes are added to words to change their part of speech. The table below lists the most common of those suffixes, the parts of speech they create, and an example of each.

Suffix	Function	Example
-ly	turns adjectives into adverbs	slow → slowly
-ify	turns adjectives into verbs	solid → solidify
-ate	turns adjectives into verbs	complex → complicate
-en	turns adjectives into verbs	soft → soften
-ize	turns nouns into verbs	pressure → pressurize
-ous	turns nouns into adjectives	prestige → prestigious
-ive	turns verbs into adjectives	select → selective
-tion	turns verbs into nouns	complicate → complication
-ment	turns verbs into nouns	embarrass → embarrassment
-ence/-ance	turns verbs into nouns	attend → attendance
-ness	turns adjectives into nouns	shy → shyness

Extend Meaning to Other Parts of Speech

When words can be used as both a noun and a verb, the meanings for the noun and verb forms of that word are generally closely related. You can probably guess what the **verb** *leech* means, since you now know what the **noun** *leech* means.

Using your knowledge of the meaning of the noun form of *leech*, pick out the definitions that you think are correct for the verb form of the word *leech*.

   a. to pick on, tease
   b. to draw or suck blood from
   c. to drain of resources, hang on like a parasite
   d. to spy on, keep an eye on

Both **b** and **c** are correct. These two answers turn the two meanings of the noun *leech* into actions. But only **c** makes sense in the context of the sentence, "Stop *leeching* off of me!"

Here's how the other meaning of the verb *leech* might work:

The doctor *leeched* the patient, hoping to draw the disease out of her body.

This sentence may sound very odd, but in the early days of medicine, it was believed that illnesses were caused by "bad blood." Many doctors believed that drawing out this bad blood would cure the patient.

SPECIAL OR LIMITED DEFINITIONS

In addition to the common, current meanings of the word, dictionary definitions often provide meanings that are:

- *Slang*
- Used only in a certain field, like biology or law
- *Archaic*

As you saw in Practice 1, *slam* has three different meanings—two when used normally and one when used as slang. Similarly, the word *person* has a special meaning when used in a legal sense. Finally, an archaic meaning is one that is no longer used. For example, the archaic meaning of the verb *leech* is "to cure or heal." But since it's an archaic meaning, you know that today's writers generally don't mean to "cure or heal" when they use *leech* as a verb.

As mentioned above, verb and noun forms of the same word are usually closely related. But words don't always follow this pattern, and you need to double check in a dictionary to be sure exactly what a word means. If you think you know what a word means but you come across it being used in a way that doesn't make sense, *look it up*. It could be that the word has a meaning you aren't aware of.

HOW TO REMEMBER NEW VOCABULARY

Of course, looking up a new word is one thing, and *remembering* it is another. Here are six strategies that can help make new, unfamiliar words a permanent part of your vocabulary.

1. **Circle the word.** If the book or text belongs to you and you can write on it, *do* write on it. Circling the word will help fix that new word and its context in your memory, and you'll be able to spot it easily whenever you come back to that sentence.

2. **Say the Word Out Loud.** Hear how the word sounds. Say it by itself and then read the whole sentence out loud to hear how the word is used.

3. **Write the Definition Down.** If possible, write the definition right there in the margin of the text. Writing the definition down will help seal it in your memory. In addition, if you can write in the text, the definition will be right there for you if you come back to the text later but have forgotten what the word means.

4. **Re-Read the Sentence.** After you know what the word means, re-read the sentence. This time you get to hear it *and* understand it.

5. **Start a Vocabulary List.** In addition to writing the definition down in the text, write it in a notebook just for vocabulary words. Write the word, its definition(s), its part of speech, and the sentence in which it is used.

6. **Use the Word in Your Own Sentence.** It's best to create your own sentence using the new word, and then write that sentence in your vocabulary notebook. If the word has more than one meaning, write a sentence for each meaning. Try to make your sentences as colorful and exciting as possible so that you'll remember the new word clearly. For example, you might write the following sentences for *leech*:

   - She screamed when she came out of the creek and saw slimy *leeches* all over her body.
   - Politicians are like *leeches*. They *leech* off of tax payers.
   - I'm sure glad doctors don't *leech* their patients anymore!

PRACTICE 3

Here's a chance to start your vocabulary list. Take out a separate sheet of paper or open up a notebook for this exercise.

- Circle each unfamiliar word in the following sentences and look it up in the dictionary. Write down its part or parts of speech.

- If there is more than one meaning for that word, write *each* definition down.
- Decide which meaning makes sense in the context of the sentence below.
- Write your own sentence for each meaning.
- If any of the definitions contain words you don't know, look those words up, too.

1. That child is often insubordinate.
2. He was exultant when he heard he'd received the award.
3. Housing developments have mushroomed in this town.
4. "I don't need to take orders from you," she replied insolently.
5. This is an abomination!

Answers

All the answers could be listed here, but it would be better for you to use an actual dictionary. Here's one answer, though, for good measure:

5. *Abomination: n.* something to be loathed.
   Loathe: v. to feel great hatred and disgust for.
   Thus, an abomination is something to feel great hatred and disgust for.
   Sentence (something I'll remember): *War is an abomination.*

In Short

To understand and remember what you read, you need to know what each word means. Always circle and look up words you don't know as soon as you come across them. Choose the meaning that matches the word's part of speech. Say new words out loud and put them on a vocabulary list. Use these new words in your own sentences to help seal their meanings in your memory.

Skill Building Until Next Time

1. Add words to your vocabulary list all week. See if you can add at least oneword a day.
2. Use your new vocabulary words in your conversations, in letters, or in other things you write this week. The more you use them, the better you'll remember them.

CHAPTER | 4

What do you do when you come across unfamiliar words but you don't have a dictionary? This chapter will show you how to use context to figure out what unfamiliar words mean.

DETERMINING MEANING FROM CONTEXT

Imagine you've applied for a job that requires a written test. You answer all the math questions with no problem, but the reading comprehension section gives you trouble. In the first passage alone, there are several words you don't know. You're not allowed to use a dictionary. What should you do?

a. Pretend you're sick, leave the room, and go find a dictionary somewhere.
b. Panic and leave everything blank.
c. Take random guesses and hope you get them right.
d. Use the context of the sentence to figure out what the words mean.

While you might be tempted to do **a**, **b**, or **c**, the smartest choice is clearly **d**. That's because unless the exam is specifically testing your vocabulary, you should be able to use the *context* of the sentences to help you determine the meaning of the word. That is, the words and sentences surrounding the unfamiliar word should give you enough clues to determine the meaning of the word. You simply need to learn how to recognize those clues.

> **What's Context?**
> Context refers to the words and ideas that surround a particular word or phrase to help express its meaning.

EXAMINING CONTEXT

Imagine you receive the following memo at work, but you don't have a dictionary handy. If you find any unfamiliar words in this memo, circle them, but don't look them up yet. Just read the memo carefully and actively.

TO: Department Managers
FROM: Herb Herbert, Office Manager
DATE: December 5, 2000
RE: Heater Distribution

As I'm sure you've noticed, the heating system has once again been behaving erratically. Yesterday the office temperature went up and down between 55 and 80 degrees. The problem was "fixed" last night, but as you know, this system has a history of recidivism. Chances are we'll have trouble again soon. Building management has promised to look into a permanent fix for this problem, but in the meantime, we should expect continued breakdowns. To keep everyone warm until then, we have ordered two dozen portable heaters. Please stop by my office this afternoon to pick up heaters for your department.

As you read, you may have come across a few unfamiliar words. Did you circle *erratically* and *recidivism*? You don't need to look these words up because if you do a little detective work, you can figure out what these words mean without the help of a dictionary. This is called **determining meaning through context**. Like a detective looking for clues at the scene of a crime, you can look in the memo for clues that will tell you what the unfamiliar words mean.

LOOK FOR CLUES

Let's start with *erratically*. In what context is this word used?

> As I'm sure you've noticed, the heating system has once again been behaving *erratically*. Yesterday the office temperature went up and down between 55 and 80 degrees.

Given these sentences, what can you tell about the word *erratically*? Well, because the heating system has been behaving erratically, the temperature wavered between 55 and 80 degrees—that's a huge range. This tells you that the heating system is not working the way it's supposed to. In addition, you know that the temperature "went up and down" between 55 and 80 degrees. That means there wasn't just one steady drop in temperature. Instead, the temperature rose and fell several times. Now, from these clues, you can probably take a pretty good guess at what *erratically* means. See if you can answer the question below.

Which of the following means the same as *erratically*?
- **a.** steadily, reliably
- **b.** irregularly, unevenly
- **c.** badly

The correct answer is **b**, *irregularly, unevenly. Erratically* clearly can't mean *steadily*, or *reliably*, because no steady or reliable heating system would range from 55 to 80 degrees in one day. Answer **c** makes sense—the system has indeed been behaving badly. But *badly* doesn't take into account the range of temperatures and the ups and downs Herb Herbert described. So **b** is the best answer and is, in fact, what *erratically* means.

Parts of Speech

The next clue is to find out what part of speech *erratically* is. You may have had to refer back to the definitions listed in Chapter 3, and that's okay, but it would be good for you to memorize the different parts of speech as soon as possible. This will make your trips to the dictionary far more productive.

The answer, by the way, is that *erratically* is an adverb. It describes an action: *how the system has been behaving*. If you looked carefully at the suffix table in Chapter 3, you might have noticed the clue that *erratically* is an adverb—it ends in *-ly*.

You probably also circled *recidivism* in the memo. What does it mean? The particular phrase in which it is used—"history of recidivism"— should tell you that *recidivism* has something to do with behavior or experience. It also tells you it's something that has been happening over a long period of time. You also know that this history of recidivism leads Herb Herbert to conclude that there will be trouble again soon. In other words, although the system has been "fixed," he expects it to go back to its old and erratic ways soon. Thus, you can assume that a history of *recidivism* means a history of which of the following?

- **a.** long-lasting, quality performance
- **b.** parts that need replacement
- **c.** repeatedly falling back into an undesirable behavior

The answer is **c**. It should be clear that answer **a** cannot be correct, because the memo says that the heating system has a history of needing fixing. It may also have parts that need replacement (answer **b**), especially since the memo says that it breaks down regularly. But the memo clearly indicates that **c** is the best answer, because every time the system is fixed, it soon goes back to having the same old problems.

Recidivism, by the way, is most commonly used to describe criminals who fall back into crime after they've served their sentence.

PRACTICE 1

1. Determine the meaning of the italicized words in the sentences below.
   - **a.** He was so nervous that his voice was *quavering*.
   - **b.** thundering, booming
   - **c.** trembling, shaking
   - **d.** quiet, whispering

2. By the time our department meeting was over at 8 P.M., I was *famished*. I had skipped lunch and hadn't eaten since breakfast.
   - **a.** famous
   - **b.** exhausted
   - **c.** starving

3. Sammy made a *bogus* phone call to the crime-stoppers hotline and pretended to be a witness to a crime.

   a. fake

   b. collect

   c. urgent

Answers

1. b

2. c

3. a

HOW MUCH CONTEXT DO YOU NEED?

In the previous example, you would still have been able to understand the main message of the memo even if you didn't know—or couldn't figure out—the meanings of *erratically* and *recidivism*. (You don't need to know what those words mean to know you should go pick up heaters for your department.) But sometimes your understanding of a passage depends upon your understanding of a particular word or phrase. Can you understand the following sentence, for example, without understanding what *affable* means?

> The new manager is a very affable person.

The trouble with adjectives like *affable* is that it can be very difficult to figure out what they mean without sufficient context. If someone describes your new manager as "affable," you'll certainly want to know what it means, but a sentence like the one above doesn't tell you much. Is *affable* something good or bad? Should you be worried or glad? No matter how good a detective you are, there simply aren't enough clues in this sentence to tell you what this word means or even whether *affable* is positive or negative. You simply need more context.

PRACTICE 2

Here is another sentence to expand the context for *affable*. Clearly *affable* is something good. Now can you determine more precisely what it means?

The new manager is a very *affable* person. Everyone likes her.

a. friendly, approachable, nice
b. pretty, good-looking
c. extremely talkative

Answer

The best answer is **a**, *friendly, approachable, nice*. The new manager may indeed be *pretty* or *extremely talkative*, but these aren't qualities that suggest everyone will like her. A friendly, approachable, nice person, however, is almost universally liked.

PRACTICE 3

For more practice, take a look at one of the most famous poems in the English language: Lewis Carroll's "Jabberwocky." (Lewis Carroll is the author of *Alice In Wonderland*.) Though you won't be able to determine *exactly* what the nonsense words in the poem mean, you should be able to take an intelligent guess at their meanings based on their context.

Below are the first two stanzas of the poem. Read them carefully and then answer the questions that follow. Read the poem twice, at least one of those times out loud. (The lines of the poem are numbered to make the questions easier to follow.)

1   'Twas brillig, and the slithy toves
2   Did gyre and gimble in the wabe;
3   All mimsy were the borogoves,
4   And the mome raths outgrabe.

5   "Beware the Jabberwock, my son!
6   The jaws that bite, the claws that catch!
7   Beware the Jubjub bird, and shun
8   The frumious Bandersnatch!"

1. What could *slithy toves* (line 1) be?
   a. some sort of food
   b. some sort of place
   c. some sort of animal

2. What is the *Jabberwock* (line 5)?

    a. a mean person

    b. a dangerous creature

    c. a harmless bird

3. What does *shun* (line 7) mean?

    a. avoid, keep away from

    b. capture

    c. make friends with

4. What could *frumious* (line 8) mean?

    a. friendly

    b. ugly

    c. dangerous

Shun, by the way, is not a nonsense word. You can find it in your dictionary.

Answers

1. c. Slithy toves could be some sort of animal. The toves "did gyre and gimble," which tells you they must be something alive and active. They could also be some sort of bug or plant, but neither of these were listed as an option.

2. b. The Jabberwock is a dangerous creature. You can tell because the speaker says to "beware the Jabberwock" and describes "the jaws that bite, the claws that catch!"

3. a. Shun means to avoid, to keep away from. It's in the dictionary!

4. c. The speaker says to shun the Bandersnatch in the same stanza as it warns against the dangerous Jabberwock and Jubjub bird. It must also be dangerous, so the listener is told to keep away from it.

IN SHORT

You can often figure out what unfamiliar words mean from the context in which they are used. Look for clues in the words and sentences surrounding unfamiliar words to help determine what they mean. Even if you can't figure out the exact meaning of a word, you should at least be able to determine whether the word means something positive or negative.

Skill Building Until Next Time

1. Before you look up any unfamiliar words this week, try to figure out what they mean from the context of the sentence or passage in which they are used. Then, look up those words in a dictionary to see if you're correct. Be sure to add these words to your vocabulary list.

2. From now on, when you write sentences for new vocabulary words, try to write sentences with contexts that make the meaning of the new words clear.

CHAPTER | 5

This chapter reviews
what you learned in
Chapters 1–4:
pre-reading strategies,
getting the facts,
using a dictionary,
and determining
meaning from context.
In this chapter, you'll
get vital practice in
using all four skills
at once.

PUTTING IT ALL TOGETHER

I f you want to become good at basketball, you can practice your dribbling, work on your jump shots, and run through your lay-ups over and over until your arms and legs ache. But you won't become really good unless you can successfully combine all of these skills on the court. Similarly, when you read, and when you want to remember what you read, you need to employ a number of different strategies at the same time. Putting together the strategies that you've learned so far will take your reading skills to the next level.

IN BRIEF

These are the strategies you've learned in the first four chapters of this book:

- **Chapter 1: Pre-Reading Strategies.** You learned the importance of "warming up" for reading tasks by breaking the text into manageable chunks and reading the pre-text. You also discovered the value of skimming ahead, jumping back, and reading aloud.
- **Chapter 2: Getting the Facts.** You practiced asking and answering the *who, what, when, where, why,* and *how* questions to find and remember the basic facts in a passage.
- **Chapter 3: Using the Dictionary.** You learned the importance of looking up each word you don't know and how to make the most of a dictionary definition. You also learned the main parts of speech, how words change when they change parts of speech, and strategies for remembering new vocabulary words.
- **Chapter 4: Determining Meaning from Context.** You practiced looking for clues to meaning in the words and sentences surrounding an unfamiliar word or phrase.

If any of these terms or strategies sound unfamiliar to you, STOP. Take a few minutes to review the chapter or concept that is unclear.

PRACTICE 1

Begin by practicing strategies from Chapters 2 and 3. Read the passage below carefully and then answer the questions that follow on a separate sheet of paper. You can use a dictionary for this exercise.

The body's nervous system is much like a complex telephone system. A network of *nerves* permeates the entire body. These nerves are made up of bundles of fibers called *neurons*. Neurons carry impulses of sensation or movement to the spinal cord and the brain. There are billions of neurons in the human body. When a cell receives an impulse, it passes the message, neuron by neuron, all the way to the brain at lightning speed.

1. Who or what is this passage about?
2. What is the nervous system like?
3. Where in the body are nerves located?
4. What are nerves?
5. What do nerves do?
6. Where do messages go?
7. How many neurons are there?
8. What does *permeate* mean?
9. What part of speech is *permeate*?
10. What would *permeable*, the adjective, mean?

Answers

1. This passage is about the nervous system.
2. The nervous system is like a complex telephone system.
3. The nerves are located everywhere in the body.
4. Nerves are bundles of neurons.
5. Nerves transmit impulses of sensation or movement.
6. Messages go to the spinal cord and brain.
7. There are billions of neurons.
8. *Permeate* means to spread or flow throughout, into every part.
9. *Permeate* is a verb.
10. *Permeable* means "able to be permeated by fluids."

If you missed	Then review
Question 1	Chapter 2
Question 2	Chapter 2
Question 3	Chapter 2
Question 4	Chapter 2
Question 5	Chapter 2
Question 6	Chapter 2
Question 7	Chapter 2
Question 8	Chapter 3
Question 9	Chapter 3
Question 10	Chapter 3

Practice 2

Now it's time to use all of the strategies you learned in Section 1 at once. Before you read the whole passage below, apply pre-reading techniques to "warm up" for the text. Then, answer the pre-reading questions below. **Don't** read the whole passage yet, and don't use a dictionary. Once you've answered the pre-reading questions, then read the entire passage. Answer the questions that follow the passage on a separate sheet of paper.

Pre-Reading Questions

1. What you're about to read is written by
   a. a student
   b. an expert
   c. a patient

2. What main topics will be covered in this passage? What key words do you expect to learn? List them below.

Give Your Back a Break
by Michael Watson, Chiropractor

Most back injuries are entirely preventable. If you keep a short list of do's and don'ts in mind, you'll be much more likely to keep your back free from injury.

Why Back Injuries Are So Common
The back is made up of 24 vertebrae, the small bones that make up the spine and protect the spinal chord. In between the vertebrae are discs, which cushion the vertebrae. The vertebrae and discs are supported by dozens of muscles and ligaments. Millions of nerve cells lead into the spinal cord, which is the main conduit for nerve messages to the brain. These nerve cells can get pinched, these muscles and ligaments can rend, and these discs can slip out of place if you don't take proper care of your back.

How to Prevent Back Injury
The number one cause of back injury is improper lifting.

Whenever you have to lift heavy objects (anything heavier than 25 pounds), be sure to use your arms and legs to do the lifting and not your back. Get down into a squatting position so that your leverage is in your legs, not your lower back muscles. If you don't bend your knees, all the strain will be on your lower back. In addition, you need to keep your back as straight as possible. Don't hunch over.

In addition, I recommend the following prevention strategies:

- Maintain a good posture. Walk, sit and stand with your back straight. This will strengthen your overall back strength and help prevent muscle strain and tears.
- Keep frequently used items within arm's reach so you don't have to stretch too far to get them.
- Don't twist as you carry heavy objects; turn your whole body instead.
- Don't stretch to reach for things above your head. Use a step ladder instead.

Post-Reading Questions

3. What are vertebrae? How many are there?
4. What does the spinal cord do?
5. What does *conduit* mean?
   a. channel, pathway
   b. home, dwelling
   c. resistance
6. What does *rend* mean?
   a. heal, mend
   b. destroy
   c. tear, rip
7. What is the main cause of back injury?
8. What's the best way to prevent back injury?
9. What part of speech is *strain* in the sentence "If you don't bend your knees, all the *strain* will be on your lower back"?

Answers

1. **b.** The passage is written by an expert.
2. The main topics are "Why back injuries are so common" and "How to prevent back injury." You should expect to learn something about the key words *vertebrae, discs, muscles,* and *ligaments*.
3. Vertebrae are the small bones in your back. There are 24 of them.
4. The spinal chord is a conduit for nerve messages to the brain.
5. **a.** A *conduit* is a channel or pathway.
6. **c.** To *rend* means to tear or rip.
7. The main cause of back injury is improper lifting.
8. The best way to prevent back injury is to lift properly.
9. In the sentence "If you don't bend your knees, all the *strain* will be on your lower back," *strain* is a noun.

If you missed	Then review
Question 1	Chapter 2
Question 2	Chapter 1
Question 3	Chapter 1
Question 4	Chapter 2
Question 5	Chapter 3
Question 6	Chapter 4
Question 7	Chapter 4
Question 8	Chapter 2
Question 9	Chapter 2
Question 10	Chapter 3

Skill Building Until Next Time

1. Review the Skill Building Until Next Time sections from each chapter this week. Try any Skill Builders you didn't do or didn't complete.
2. Write a paragraph about what you've learned this week. Try to use at least one vocabulary word you've learned this week in your paragraph.

SECTION 2

GETTING—AND REMEMBERING—THE GIST OF IT

Writers write for a reason: They have a specific idea they want to convey. Good writers use facts and other kinds of evidence to support their idea. As a reader, you need to be able to identify that main idea and distinguish between the main idea and its support. You should also be able to distinguish between different levels of supporting ideas. These skills will help you determine which ideas are most important—and therefore which ideas you need to remember.

The chapters in this section will teach you how to identify and remember key words, facts, and ideas. Specifically, you'll learn how to:

- Find the main idea
- Find supporting ideas
- Underline, highlight, and gloss the text
- Take notes and outline your reading material

CHAPTER | 6

Finding and understanding the *main* idea of a text is an essential reading skill. This chapter will show you how to distinguish the main idea from its support.

FINDING THE MAIN IDEA

Finding and understanding the *main* idea of a text is an essential reading skill. This chapter will show you how to distinguish the main idea from its support.

Imagine that one of your coworkers has just handed you something to read. "What's it about?" you ask. You'd like to know what to expect when you sit down to read. But your question won't really get you the answer you're looking for. That's because you've only asked about the *subject* of the text. The subject—what a text is *about*—is only half the story.

When writers write, it's always for a reason. They have something they want to write *about*, and they have something they want to say *about* that subject. When you look beyond the facts and information to what the writer really wants to say *about* his subject, you're looking for the *main idea*.

Thus, you can have ten different things to read about home computers, but each of these texts can be as different as New York City is from Wakita, Kansas, because they can all have completely different main ideas.

HOW THE MAIN IDEA WORKS

Let's take a look at a sample paragraph to see exactly how the main idea works. Read the passage below carefully and answer the question that follows:

> The demand for health care workers is on the rise. The government's Bureau of Labor Statistics (BLS) reports that employment in health service industries through the year 2005 will grow at almost double the rate of all other (non-farm) wage and salary employment. In sheer numbers, about 9 million American workers are now employed in health services. By 2005, that number is expected to be at about 13 million—an increase of nearly 4 million jobs.

1. What is the main idea of this paragraph?

What's a Main Idea?
A main idea is the overall fact, feeling, or thought a writer wants to convey about her subject.

If you answered "jobs in health care," it's a good start, but not quite right. You've identified the subject of this passage. But you've also confused the *subject* with the *main idea*. "Jobs in health care" is what the paragraph is *about*, but it's not what the writer wants to say *about* that subject. It's not the *main idea*. The main idea is what the writer has to say *about* jobs in health care. Thus, the correct answer to the question, the main idea of the paragraph, is this:

The demand for health care workers is on the rise.

This sentence expresses the main idea because it shows both what the subject is *and* what's important or interesting *about* that subject. It also tells readers that they should expect to learn about this increased demand for health care workers in the rest of the paragraph. A writer's job is not only to make his or her main idea clear but also to support that main idea.

A main idea says something about the subject, but there's more. A main idea must also have the following characteristics:

1. It must be *general* enough to encompass all of the ideas in the passage.
2. It must be *an assertion.*

Main Ideas Are General

The main idea of a passage must be something that is *general enough* to encompass all of the ideas in the passage. That is, it should be broad enough that all of the other sentences in the passage fit underneath it like people under an umbrella. For example, look again at the paragraph about the demand for health care workers re-printed below. The first sentence states the *general* main idea. Then each sentence that follows gives *specific* facts and statistics to *support* that main idea. These sentences provide specific evidence to show that the main idea is valid or true. They all fit under the "umbrella" of the larger idea—that the demand for health care workers is on the rise.

> The demand for health care workers is on the rise. The government's Bureau of Labor Statistics (BLS) reports that employment in health service industries through the year 2005 will grow at almost double the rate of all other (non-farm) wage and salary employment. In sheer numbers, about 9 million American workers are now employed in health services. By 2005, that number is expected to be at about 13 million—an increase of nearly 4 million jobs.

PRACTICE 1

In each group of sentences below, which sentence is general enough to be the main idea?

Group A
1. Hundreds of thousands of people were killed during the decades of fighting.
2. The African country of Angola is still feeling the effects of its long and bloody civil war.

3. The civil war, which lasted 19 years, finally ended in 1994.
4. Though the government is officially in control, UNITAS rebel forces still hold over half of the country's territory.

Group B
1. There were only 15 work-related accidents last year.
2. Previous years show an average of 30 accidents per year.
3. This drop is largely due to the new "Checks and Balances Safety System."
4. The number of work-related accidents has dropped by 50 percent this year.

Answers
Group A
In group A only sentence number **2** is general enough to be the main idea. Notice how the other sentences give specific details about the Angolan civil war and therefore fit under sentence 2's umbrella.

Group B
In Group B, only sentence number **4** is general enough to be the main idea. It does provide a specific percentage (50 percent). But notice how all the other sentences give specific details about *how* and *why* the number of accidents dropped by 50 percent. Thus, sentences 1–3 fit under the umbrella of sentence 4.

Main Ideas Are Assertions

The main idea must also be some kind of *assertion* about the subject. An *assertion* is a claim that needs to be supported with specific details or evidence. Even matters of fact (things that are known to be true) can be assertions. The assertion "The demand for health care workers is on the rise" works as a main idea because it is a general assertion that needs some supporting details to *show* that it is true. In other words, the main idea *tells* readers that something is true. The supporting sentences, on the other hand, *show* that it's true by providing specific facts and details.

What's an Assertion?
An *assertion* is a claim that requires evidence or support in order for it to be accepted as true.

PRACTICE 2

Which of the following are assertions that require evidence or support?

1. Red is a primary color.
2. Red is the prettiest color.
3. Employees may work overtime.
4. Company policy states that employees must have permission to work more than 10 hours of overtime.
5. We should get paid more for overtime.
6. Fewer employees working more overtime hours would cost more than more employees working fewer overtime hours.

Answers

Sentences **2**, **5**, and **6** are assertions that require support. Sentences **1**, **3**, and **4**, on the other hand, are simple statements of fact that do not require support.

TOPIC SENTENCES AND WHERE TO FIND THEM

Writers often state their main idea in one or two sentences so that readers can be very clear about the main point of the text. A sentence that expresses the main idea of a paragraph is called a **topic sentence**. In the paragraph about health care workers, the first sentence expresses the main idea; it is the topic sentence for the paragraph.

Topic sentences are often found at the beginning of paragraphs. But not all paragraphs begin with a clear topic sentence. Sometimes writers begin with specific supporting ideas that lead up to the main idea. In this case, the topic sentence is often found at the end of the paragraph. Here's an example:

When I was in kindergarten, I wanted to be an astronaut. When I was in junior high school, I wanted to be a doctor. When I was in high school, I wanted to be a teacher. Today, I'm 35 and I'm a firefighter. I had a lot of career goals

What's a Topic Sentence?
A sentence in a paragraph that clearly expresses a writer's main idea is called a topic sentence.

when I was growing up, but none of them correspond to what I actually turned out to be.

Notice how the last sentence in the paragraph is the only sentence that serves as an umbrella for all of the other sentences in the paragraph.

Sometimes the topic sentence is not found at the beginning or end of a paragraph but rather somewhere in the middle. And in still other cases, there won't be a clear topic sentence at all. But that doesn't mean there is no main idea. It's there, but the author has chosen not to express it in a clear topic sentence. In this case, you have to look carefully at the paragraph for clues about the main idea. You'll tackle this situation in Chapter 18.

MAIN IDEAS IN PARAGRAPHS AND ESSAYS

When readers talk about a text (an article, memo, or book, for example), they generally claim it has *one* main idea. But if it has more than one paragraph, shouldn't it have as many main ideas as it has paragraphs? Yes and no. Each paragraph should indeed have its own main idea. In fact, that's the definition of a paragraph: a group of sentences about the same idea. At the same time, however, each paragraph does something more. It works to support the main idea of the *entire passage*. Thus, there is an *overall* main idea (often called a *theme* or *thesis*) for the text. The main idea *of each paragraph* should work to support the overall main idea of the entire text (you'll find a diagram of this structure in the next chapter).

PRACTICE 3

Look again at the following passage from Chapter 3. (The paragraphs are numbered to make the questions easier to follow.) Re-read the passage carefully to find the main idea. Remember that the main idea should both make an assertion about the subject and be general enough to hold together all of the ideas in the paragraph.

(1) According to a recent study conducted by Elmont Community College, distance learning is a legitimate alternative to traditional classroom education.

(2) In February, the college surveyed 1,000 adults across the country to see if distance learning programs were meeting

the needs of the students. Five hundred of those surveyed were enrolled in traditional, on-campus classes and 500 were enrolled in "virtual" classes that "met" online through the Internet. These online classes were offered by 29 different universities. All students surveyed were in degree programs.

What's a Paragraph?
A *paragraph* is a group of sentences about the same idea.

(3) A large majority of the distance learning students—87 percent—said they were satisfied with their learning experience. "This was a much higher percentage than we expected," said Karen Kaplan, director of the study. In fact, it was just short of the 88 percent of traditional classroom students who claimed they were satisfied.

(4) In addition, many distance learning students reported that the flexibility and convenience of the virtual environment was more important to them than face-to-face interaction with classmates and instructors. While they missed the human contact, they really needed the ability to attend class any time of day or night. This is largely due to the fact that nearly all distance learning students—96 percent—hold full-time jobs, compared to only 78 percent of adult students enrolled in traditional classes.

What's a Thesis?
The overall main idea for a whole text (such as an article, essay, or memo) is often called a *thesis.*

1. What is the *subject* of this passage?
2. What is the *main idea* of paragraph 2?
3. What is the *main idea* of paragraph 3?
4. What is the *main idea* of paragraph 4?
5. What is the *overall main idea* of the passage?

Answers

1. The subject of this passage is distance learning.
2. The main idea of paragraph #2 is: The college surveyed 1,000 students to see how distance learning compared to regular classroom learning. This idea is expressed in the first sentence of that paragraph.

3. The main idea of paragraph #3 is: 87 percent of the distance learning students were satisfied. This idea is expressed in the first sentence of that paragraph.

4. The main idea of paragraph #4 is: The flexibility and convenience were very important to distance learning students. This idea, again, is expressed in the first sentence of that paragraph.

5. The overall main idea of the passage is expressed clearly in the second part of the very first sentence: "distance learning is a legitimate alternative to traditional classroom education." This is the idea that the main ideas from all of the other paragraphs add up to. Just like the main idea in a paragraph has to be general enough to cover all the ideas in the paragraph, the overall main idea has to be general enough to encompass all of the ideas in the passage. The main ideas in paragraphs 2, 3, and 4 all work to support this overall main idea.

HOW MAIN IDEAS HELP YOU REMEMBER

The main idea is the most important part of a paragraph or passage, and it is therefore the most important thing to remember. That's why it's so important to be able to identify the main idea of whatever you read. The main idea gives you a *context* in which to place the specific facts and ideas expressed in the rest of the paragraph. That is, it gives you a framework for understanding the rest of the passage—a sense of "here's what it all adds up to."

IN SHORT

Main ideas have three characteristics:

1. They say something *about* the subject.
2. They make an *assertion* about the subject.
3. They are general.

Main ideas are often expressed in clear topic sentences and are accompanied by sentences that offer specific support. In longer texts, each paragraph has a main idea, and each main idea works to support the main idea of the whole passage. Finding the main idea will help you focus on what to remember and give facts and details a context.

Skill Building Until Next Time

1. As you read today and throughout the week, notice how texts are divided into paragraphs of sentences about the same idea. See if there's a topic sentence that expresses the main idea and holds each paragraph together.
2. Create topic sentences about things you come across in your day. Make general assertions about people, places, and things. For example, you might say, "Kreme Kakes makes better donuts than Donuts-to-Go!" Then, support your assertion. Does the brand you prefer have more flavor? Less fat? Less grease? Cost less?

CHAPTER | 7

Because main ideas are assertions, they need support. This chapter explains the types of support writers use. You'll also learn how to distinguish between major and minor supporting ideas, which will help you focus on what to remember.

FINDING THE SUPPORTING IDEAS

The main idea of a paragraph is like an umbrella that "covers" the rest of the sentences in the paragraph. The other sentences in the paragraph offer *support* for the main idea. But what exactly is that support? How does it work? And why does it matter?

You might think of a piece of writing as a table. The top of the table is the main idea—what the writer thinks, believes, or knows about her subject. But the table won't stand without legs to support it. In writing, those "legs" are the specific facts and ideas that support the main idea. They are the "proof" or "evidence" writers provide to *show* that their main idea is valid.

TYPES OF SUPPORT

Writers support their ideas in a variety of ways. They often use a combination of the following types of specific support:

- details
- facts
- examples
- explanations
- definitions
- comparisons
- quotations
- statistics
- descriptions
- reasons

For example, imagine you receive the following memo regarding tuition reimbursement at work. Read it carefully and then look at the way it is outlined below. The sentences are numbered to make the passage easier to analyze.

(1) Due to increasing costs, there will be two changes in the tuition reimbursement program that will significantly reduce employee benefits. (2) First, reimbursement has been reduced from 100 percent to 60 percent of tuition costs for each course in which the student earns a "C" or better. (3) For example, if you pay $1,000 for a course, and earn at least a C in that course, you will be reimbursed in the amount of $600. (4) Second, employees will now be limited to $2,000 in reimbursement expenses per year. (5) Thus, if your tuition per course equals $1,000, you will be reimbursed $600 per course for each of your three courses but only $200 for the fourth course because you will have reached the $2,000 limit. (6) Any additional courses in that year will not be reimbursed.

This paragraph follows a very common pattern. It starts with the topic sentence (sentence 1). Then it offers support for that topic sentence in the form of *details* and *examples*. Sentences 2 and 4 give the details of the change in the tuition reimbursement program. Sentences 3, 5, and 6 give specific examples of those changes. Thus, the organization looks like this (sentence numbers are in parentheses):

Main idea (**1**)
   Detail (**2**)
        Example (**3**)
   Detail (**4**)
        Example (**5, 6**)

DISTINGUISHING MAIN IDEAS FROM SUPPORTING IDEAS

If you're not sure whether something is a *main* idea or *supporting* idea, ask yourself whether the sentence is making a general statement or providing specific information. In the tuition reimbursement memo, notice how all of the sentences besides Sentence 1 are making very specific statements. They are not general enough to serve as an umbrella for the whole paragraph. Therefore, they must be working to support the main idea.

Signal Words

You can often tell whether a sentence is expressing a main idea or providing support by looking for certain clues. Notice how each supporting sentence from the memo begins:

Sentence 2:	First, …
Sentence 3:	For example, …
Sentence 4:	Second, …
Sentence 5:	Thus, …

These words and others like them are *signal words*: They tell you that a supporting fact or idea will follow. The following list shows some of the most common words and phrases that *signal* supporting ideas.

Transitions		
accordingly	however	next
also	in additionon	the other hand
as a result	indeed	secondly
first	in fact	since
first of all	in other words	specifically
for example	inparticular	then
for instance	likewise	therefore
furthermore	nevertheless	thus

These signal words and phrases are often called *transitions*. Transitions are words and phrases that writers use to move from one idea to the next. They show the relationships between ideas so that readers can see how ideas are connected. In other words, these transitions help show readers how ideas work together to support the main idea in a passage. For example, the transitional word *likewise* shows that the ideas before and after it are similar; they have something in common. The transitional phrase *for example* tells readers that what comes next is an example of what came before. That's how transitions work.

What are Transitions?
Transitions are words and phrases that signal a shift from one idea to the next or show how ideas are related.

Sentence A	→ *likewise* → ↓ Shows that there are similarities between the ideas in Sentences A and B.	Sentence B
Sentence A	→ *for example* → ↓ Shows that Sentence B provides an example of the idea in Sentence A.	Sentence B

PRACTICE 1

Read the paragraph below carefully. Underline any words or phrases that signal a supporting idea.

> Our new marketing campaign has been a tremendous success. In fact, since we've been advertising on the radio, sales have increased by 35%. Likewise, our client references have doubled, and we've improved our client retention rates. Furthermore, we've had to hire five new sales representatives to meet demand.

Answer

> Our new marketing campaign has been a tremendous success. <u>In fact</u>, since we've been advertising on the radio, sales have increased by 35%. <u>Likewise</u>, our client references have doubled, and we've improved our client retention rates. <u>Furthermore</u>, we've had to hire five new sales representatives to meet demand.

Two Questions to Ask

To help you distinguish between main and supporting ideas, then, there are two questions you can ask:

1. Is the idea general enough to be a main idea, or is it a specific detail?
2. Is there a transitional word or phrase indicating that it's probably a supporting idea? Sometimes just one question will make it clear, but be careful. Not every sentence will have a signal word or phrase to tell you that it's a supporting sentence. Also, you need to be careful to distinguish which main idea a supporting idea actually supports.

PRACTICE 2

Read the following passage carefully and then answer the questions that follow (the paragraphs are numbered to make the questions easier to follow).

(1) Citizens of Montgomery County, vote no on the referendum for local tax reform! The referendum will actually do the *opposite* of what it promises.

(2) First of all, the referendum will not reduce taxes for middle income families. In fact, middle income families with children will pay 10 percent *more* per year, and 20 percent more if they don't have children.

(3) Second, the referendum actually *decreases* taxes for the wealthiest tax bracket. In fact, taxpayers in the highest bracket will pay 10 percent *less* per year if the referendum is passed.

(4) VOTE NO on Tuesday!

1. In this passage, what is the sentence "Second, the referendum actually *decreases* taxes for the wealthiest tax bracket"?
    a. It's the main idea of the whole passage.
    b. It's the main idea of paragraph 3.
    c. It's a supporting idea for the main idea of the whole passage.
    d. It's a supporting idea for paragraph 3.
2. In the passage, what is the sentence "In fact, middle income families with children will pay 10 percent more per year, and 20 percent more if they don't have children"?
    a. It's the main idea of paragraph 2.
    b. It's a fact that supports the main idea of paragraph 2.

3. What is the other sentence that supports the overall main idea of the passage?

Answers

1. The correct answer is both **b** and **c**. "Second" is a signal word that indicates the sentence has a supporting idea. But what is it supporting? Is it supporting the main idea in paragraph 3? No. It can't be, because it *is* the main idea of paragraph 3. So what is it supporting? It must be supporting the main idea of the whole text: "The referendum will actually do the *opposite* of what it promises.

2. b. The second sentence in paragraph 2 is a fact that supports the main idea of paragraph 2. The transition "in fact" should signal this relationship.

3. The first sentence of paragraph 2, "First of all, the referendum will not reduce taxes for middle income families," is the other idea that directly supports the overall main idea.

LEVELS OF SUPPORT

As you can see by now, there are often several different levels of support in a passage. A major supporting idea is one that directly supports the overall main idea. A minor supporting idea, on the other hand, offers support for a major supporting idea. Look at it this way:

I. Overall main idea (thesis)

    A. Major Supporting Idea (directly supports thesis)
        1. Minor supporting idea (supports idea A)
        2. Minor supporting idea (supports idea A)
        3. Minor supporting idea (supports idea A)

    B. Major Supporting Idea (directly supports thesis)
        1. Minor supporting idea (supports idea B)
        2. Minor supporting idea (supports idea B)
        3. Minor supporting idea (supports idea B)

    C. Major Supporting Idea (directly supports thesis)
        1. Minor supporting idea (supports idea C)
        2. Minor supporting idea (supports idea C)
        3. Minor supporting idea (supports idea C)

This pattern can work in a single paragraph as well as in a larger text. That is, within the same paragraph, there can be major and minor supporting ideas for that paragraph's main idea.

Whether a passage has only major supporting ideas or both major and minor supporting ideas often makes a difference in how strong or helpful that passage is. For example, look at the version of the memo regarding tuition reimbursement that is reprinted here. This time, the memo includes only *major* supporting ideas:

> (1) Due to increasing costs, there will be two changes in the tuition reimbursement program that will significantly reduce employee benefits. (2) First, reimbursement has been reduced from 100 percent to 60 percent of tuition costs for each course in which the student earns a "C" or better. (3) Second, employees will now be limited to $2,000 in reimbursement expenses per year.

Notice how this paragraph gives readers the major details they need—the changes in the tuition reimbursement program. This is the most important information readers need to know. But *minor* supporting details make the paragraph more effective by providing specific examples. Notice how much more helpful the paragraph is with the minor support—the specific examples—reinserted. Not only is it more helpful to have minor supporting ideas, it also makes the information about the changes easier to remember by making the ideas more concrete. Here's the complete paragraph once more. The major supporting sentences are in italics and the minor supporting ideas are in bold:

> (1) Due to increasing costs, there will be two changes in the tuition reimbursement program that will significantly reduce employee benefits. (2) *First, reimbursement has been reduced from 100 percent to 60 percent of tuition costs for each course in which the student earns a "C" or better.* (3) **For example, if you pay $1,000 for a course, and earn at least a C in that course, you will be reimbursed in the amount of $600.** (4) *Second, employees will now be limited to $2,000 in reimbursement expenses per year.* (5) **Thus, if your tuition per course equals $1,000, you will be reimbursed $600 per course for each of your three courses but only $200 for the fourth course because you will have reached the $2,000 limit.** (6) **Any additional courses in that year will not be reimbursed.**

Here's the same paragraph in outline form:

I. Due to increasing costs, there will be two changes in the tuition reimbursement program that will significantly reduce employee benefits.
   A. First, reimbursement has been reduced from 100 percent to 60 percent of tuition costs for each course in which the student earns a "C" or better.
      1. For example, if you pay $1,000 for a course, and earn at least a C in that course, you will be reimbursed in the amount of $600.
   B. Second, employees will now be limited to $2,000 in reimbursement expenses per year.
      1. Thus, if your tuition per course equals $1,000, you will be reimbursed $600 per course for each of your three courses but only $200 for the fourth course because you will have reached the $2,000 limit.
      2. Any additional courses in that year will not be reimbursed.

PRACTICE 3

Here's another passage with major and minor support. Read it carefully and answer the questions that follow. As you read, see if you can determine:

1. The overall main idea
2. The main idea of each paragraph (major supporting ideas)
3. Minor supporting ideas

Be careful—the overall main idea is not where you might expect it to be. The sentences are numbered to make the questions easier to answer.

   (1) A new mandatory drug testing policy will take effect at our Detroit office on July 1st. (2) Under this new policy, all employees will be required to take a urine test four times throughout the year. (3) These tests will be unannounced. (4) Employees who refuse to take the tests will be automatically suspended without pay.

(5) An employee who tests positive for substance abuse will face several consequences. (6) To start, the employee will be immediately suspended without pay. (7) In addition, the employee must issue a statement explaining how he or she tested positive for illegal substances. (8) Then, a three-member employee panel will be assigned to review the employee's case. (9) A "typical" violator might be permitted to return to work on probationary status and be required to attend counseling.

(10) The new drug testing policy may seem strict, but it is designed to improve the health and safety of all employees of Data Management Co. (11) Indeed, our attempt to create a drug-free workplace is modeled after the programs that have improved overall workplace safety for other companies around the country. (12) Furthermore, we feel that a drug-free workplace will improve employee morale while it reduces sick days and down time.

(13) As part of the policy, we have added a counselor to our staff. (14) Dr. Jennifer Jenkins has extensive experience as a workplace counselor, particularly in dealing with substance abuse. (15) Her office is located next to Denise Robinson's in Human Resources.

1. What is the overall main idea?
2. Which sentences contain major supporting ideas?
3. Which sentences contain minor supporting ideas?
4. Circle or underline all signal words and phrases you can find.

Answers

1. The overall main idea of this passage is found in sentence **10**: "The new drug testing policy may seem strict, but it is designed to improve the health and safety of all employees of Data Management Co." This sentence makes a general statement about the mandatory drug testing policy and its purpose. It's an idea that can serve as an umbrella for the whole text. All of the other ideas in this passage give specific details about how the policy will work, how violators will be tested, and how the policy will improve safety.

2. Sentences **1, 5,** and **13** express major supporting ideas.

3. Sentences **2, 3, 4, 6, 7, 8, 9, 11, 12, 14,** and **15** all offer minor supporting details.

4. Here are the middle paragraphs with their signal words in bold:

> (5) An employee who tests positive for substance abuse will face several consequences. (6) **To start**, the employee will be immediately suspended without pay. (7) **In addition**, the employee must issue a statement explaining how he or she tested positive for illegal substances. (8) **Then**, a three-member employee panel will be assigned to review the employee's case. (9) A "typical" violator might be permitted to return to work on probationary status and be required to attend counseling.
>
> (10) The new drug testing policy may seem strict, but it is designed to improve the health and safety of all employees of Data Management Co. (11) **Indeed**, our attempt to create a drug-free workplace is modeled after the programs that have improved overall workplace safety for other companies around the country. (12) **Furthermore**, we feel that a drug-free workplace will improve employee morale while it reduces sick days and down time.

In Short

Supporting ideas "hold up" their main ideas like legs support a table. They offer facts, examples, definitions, and so on to support the main idea. That is, supporting ideas serve as "evidence" that the main idea is valid or true. Supporting ideas are often introduced by specific transitional words and phrases like "for example." Writers often use a combination of major and minor supporting ideas to support their main idea.

Skill Building Until Next Time

1. Notice how you support your ideas and assertions when you speak with others, especially if you're trying to convince them of something. How much support do you offer? What kind?
2. Look for supporting ideas in things that you read throughout the week. How much support does the writer provide? Can you tell the difference between major and minor supporting ideas?

CHAPTER | 8

When you have a lot
to read and a lot to
remember, three active
reading strategies will
help you focus on the most
information that's most
important. This chapter
will show you how to
effectively *highlight,*
underline, and *gloss*
what you read.

HIGHLIGHTING, UNDERLINING, AND GLOSSING

You know how to determine the main idea. You know how to find supporting ideas and even how to distinguish between major and minor support. But once you're done reading, how do you *remember* all of these ideas? The three active reading strategies discussed in this chapter—*highlighting, underlining,* and *glossing*—will show you how to keep track of what you read.

HIGHLIGHTING AND UNDERLINING

Whenever possible, active readers *write* on and around the texts they read. Two of the most helpful mark-up strategies are *highlighting* and *underlining*. These two strategies have the same goal: to mark important words, phrases, and ideas so that they stand out from the rest of the text. Highlighting and underlining make key words and ideas easier to see and remember.

The key to effective highlighting and underlining is to *be selective*. If you highlight every other word or sentence, you defeat your purpose. Too much will be highlighted and nothing will stand out.

So how do you know what's important enough to highlight? Part of it is simply relying on your judgment. Which ideas matter to you? What seems most interesting or important? But another question to ask is, is it a major or minor supporting idea? In general, when you're reading to remember, you should focus on main ideas and their major support. If you remember minor supporting ideas as well, terrific—but it's usually not essential, and trying to remember too many minor supporting ideas will increase the chances you'll forget the major ones. Thus, as a general rule, major supporting ideas should be underlined, and minor ones should not.

> **Highlighting**
> Highlighting is most effective if you're selective. Highlight only what's most important.

Another factor to consider is the context in which you're reading. Will you be tested on the information or the text? Are you reading for your own self-improvement or knowledge? Or both? If you're reading for a test situation, then highlighting will help, but you'll have the most success if you use highlighting or underlining in conjunction with other active reading strategies like outlining or note-taking. These techniques are covered in Chapter 9.

Highlighting and underlining will benefit you most when you use them, not abuse them. Here are some general guidelines for highlighting and underlining. What you actually highlight or underline will vary depending upon the length and type of text you're reading, of course.

- Highlight or underline the overall main idea.
- Highlight or underline major supporting ideas.
- Highlight or underline any key words defined in the text.

- Highlight or underline facts or ideas that you find particularly interesting or important
- If there are several key points in a series, number those key points.

WHEN TO HIGHLIGHT AND UNDERLINE

When you highlight or underline generally depends upon your intentions. One option is to highlight or underline *as* you read. But this is not always the most effective strategy. You should do this only if you plan to go back and take notes or write an outline. Then your highlighting or underlining will serve as a guide when you go back to take notes.

The trouble with highlighting or underlining *as* you read is that you might highlight or underline ideas that prove to be minor details once you see the whole picture. It may have seemed important at the time, but now that you've finished reading, you see it's not so important after all. Or, vice versa: If you highlight or underline as you read, you might not mark important ideas because they didn't seem so important on your first read through.

> **Read It Twice**
> Read the text twice—first to understand, then to highlight and remember.

That's why you should read through the text first without highlighting or underlining. Then, once you have gone through the text and have a sense of the big picture, it will be easier to go back and highlight or underline what's important.

Of course, reading a text twice takes time. But it's time well spent. If you read *first* to understand and then *read again* to highlight what's important, you'll understand and remember more.

PRACTICE 1

Take a look at the following passage to practice highlighting and underlining strategies. The first paragraph should look familiar to you. Read the passage carefully. Then go back and highlight or underline according to the general rules listed above.

The first paragraph has been highlighted (in bold) for you as an example. Notice the topic sentence is highlighted as well as two important supporting facts: that the jobs "will grow at almost double the rate" of other jobs and that there will be "an increase of nearly 4 million jobs." Notice how highlighting these key facts and ideas makes the paragraph more manageable. (The last section that's highlighted, "an increase of nearly 4 million jobs," may seem like a minor supporting fact to you. But because it's a nice clear statistic, it's easy and important to remember, and it helps make sense of "double the rate.") Also, notice that you do not have to highlight complete sentences.

A Bright, Bright Future

The demand for health care workers is on the rise. The government's Bureau of Labor Statistics (BLS) reports that employment in health service industries through the year 2005 **will grow at almost double the rate** of all other (non-farm) wage and salary employment. In sheer numbers, about 9 million American workers are now employed in health services. By 2005, that number is expected to be at about 13 million—**an increase of nearly 4 million jobs.**

Within the allied health field in particular, prospects are looking good. Allied health embraces a wide range of careers—surgical technicians, dieticians, licensed practical nurses (LPNs), genetic counselors, and dental hygienists, to name a few. The fact is, employment in the vast majority of all allied health occupations is expected to increase at a much faster than average rate—at least 27 to 40 percent—through the year 2005.

A primary factor contributing to the rosy outlook for allied health professionals is the "managed care" system taking root in the healthcare industry today. Health maintenance organizations (HMOs) offer a perfect example of managed care. HMOs operate by setting fixed fees for health-care services provided under their plans. If those needs are met for less, that extra money becomes profitable for the HMO. In other words, the doctors don't decide what to charge for their services—the HMOs do. And oftentimes it simply costs less, without sacrificing quality care, to get an allied health professional to do certain things the doctor used to do.

This doesn't mean doctors are going out of business. It means they're shifting their focus more toward the services only they are trained to do and leaving a broad range of services to other capable hands. Under managed care systems, more and more emphasis is being placed on pre-care and post-care which means placing more and more responsibility for healthcare delivery in the hands of allied health workers.

Answer

There is no one right answer to this exercise because there are many ways to highlight this passage effectively. In general, though, there shouldn't be much more highlighting or underlining than what you see here. If your passage looks significantly different, take a close look at what you chose to highlight. Are they major or minor supporting ideas? Why did you highlight them? Why do you think they are not highlighted in this answer?

Within the allied health field in particular, prospects are looking good. Allied health embraces a **wide range of careers**—surgical technicians, dieticians, licensed practical nurses (LPNs), genetic counselors, and dental hygienists, to name a few. The fact is, employment in the vast majority of all allied health occupations is **expected to increase at a much faster than average rate**—at least 27 to 40 percent—through the year 2005.

A primary factor contributing to the rosy outlook for allied health professionals is the "managed care" system taking root in the healthcare industry today. Health maintenance organizations (HMOs) offer a perfect example of managed care. HMOs operate by setting fixed fees for healthcare services provided under their plans. If those needs are met for less, that extra money becomes profitable for the HMO. In other words, the doctors don't decide what to charge for their services—the HMOs do. And **oftentimes it simply costs less,** without sacrificing quality care, **to get an allied health professional to do certain things the doctor used to do.**

This doesn't mean **doctors** are going out of business. It means **they're shifting their focus more toward the services only they are trained to do and leaving a broad range of**

services to other capable hands. Under managed care system, more and more emphasis is being placed on pre-care and post-care, which means placing more and more responsibility for healthcare delivery in the hands of allied health workers.

PRACTICE 2

Try highlighting another passage now. Keep in mind the highlighting and underlining guidelines mentioned earlier. First read the passage carefully, and then go back and highlight or underline it.

There are three different kinds of burns: first degree, second degree, and third degree. Each type of burn requires a different type of medical treatment.

The least serious burn is the first degree burn. This burn causes the skin to turn red but does not cause blistering. A mild sunburn is a good example of a first degree burn, and, like a mild sunburn, first degree burns generally do not require medical treatment other than a gentle cooling of the burned skin with ice or cold tap water.

Second degree burns, on the other hand, do cause blistering of the skin and should be treated immediately. These burns should be immersed in warm water and then wrapped in a sterile dressing or bandage. (Do not apply butter or grease to these burns; despite the old wives' tale, butter does not help burns heal and actually increases the chances of infection.) If second degree burns cover a large part of the body, then the victim should be taken to the hospital immediately for medical care.

Third degree burns are those that char the skin and turn it black or burn so deeply that the skin shows white. These burns usually result from direct contact with flames and have a great chance of becoming infected. All third degree burn victims should receive immediate hospital care. Burns should not be immersed in water, and charred clothing should not be removed from the victim as it may also remove skin. If possible, a sterile dressing or bandage should be applied to burns before the victim is transported to the hospital.

Answer

Again, there will be variations, but here's one way to highlight the passage:

> **There are three different kinds of burns:** first degree, second degree, and third degree. **Each type of burn requires a different type of medical treatment.**
>
> The least serious burn is the **first degree burn.** This burn **causes the skin to turn red but does not cause blistering.** A mild sunburn is a good example of a first degree burn, and, like a mild sunburn, first degree burns **generally do not require medical treatment** other than a gentle cooling of the burned skin with ice or cold tap water.
>
> **Second degree burns,** on the other hand, do **cause blistering of the skin and should be treated immediately.** These burns should **be immersed in warm water and then wrapped in a sterile dressing or bandage.** (Do not apply butter or grease to these burns; despite the old wives' tale, butter does not help burns heal and actually increases the chances of infection.) If second degree burns cover a large part of the body, then the victim should be taken to the hospital immediately for medical care.
>
> **Third degree burns** are those that **char the skin and turn it black or burn so deeply that the skin shows white.** These burns usually result from direct contact with flames and have a great chance of becoming infected. **All third degree burn victims should receive immediate hospital care.** Burns should not be immersed in water, and charred clothing should not be removed from the victim as it may also remove skin. If possible, a sterile dressing or bandage should be applied to burns before the victim is transported to the hospital.

GLOSSING

Glossing is another active reading strategy that will help you remember the key ideas in what you read. There are two steps in the glossing process:

- Read the text carefully.
- In the margin, next to each paragraph, *copy or summarize the main idea* of each paragraph.

If you don't own the text and can't write in it, you can still gloss on a separate piece of paper. The most difficult part of glossing is deciding exactly what to write in the margin. For the passage you highlighted in Practice 2, for example, you could gloss the paragraph as follows:

Different kinds of burns	There are three different kinds of burns: first degree, second degree, and third degree. Each type of burn requires a different type of medical treatment.
First degree burns	The least serious burn is the first degree burn. This burn causes the skin to turn red but does not cause blistering. A mild sunburn is a good example of a first degree burn, and, like a mild sunburn, first degree burns generally do not require medical treatment other than a gentle cooling of the burned skin with ice or cold tap water.
Second degree burns	Second degree burns, on the other hand, do cause blistering of the skin and should be treated immediately. These burns should be immersed in warm water and then wrapped in a sterile dressing or bandage. (Do not apply butter or grease to these burns; despite the old wives' tale, butter does not help burns heal and actually increases the chances of infection.) If second degree burns cover a large part of the body, then the victim should be taken to the hospital immediately for medical care.
Third degree burns	Third degree burns are those that char the skin and turn it black or burn so deeply that the skin shows white. These burns usually result from direct contact with flames and have a great chance of becoming infected. All third degree burn victims should receive immediate hospital care. Burns should not be immersed in water, and charred clothing should not be removed from the victim as it may also remove skin. If possible, a sterile dressing or bandage should be applied to burns before the victim is transported to the hospital.

But this kind of glossing doesn't do much for memory or understanding. Can you guess why? This glossing only gives the *subjects* of each paragraph. The notes in the margins don't say anything *about* those subjects, so you don't know what's important to remember.

A much better glossing would look more like the following:

Different burns require dif. care	There are three different kinds of burns: first degree, second degree, and third degree. Each type of burn requires a different type of medical treatment.
1st degree: no blistering and no medical treatment	The least serious burn is the first degree burn. This burn causes the skin to turn red but does not cause blistering. A mild sunburn is a good example of a first degree burn, and, like a mild sunburn, first degree burns generally do not require medical treatment other than a gentle cooling of the burned skin with ice or cold tap water.
2nd degree: blistering, treat immediately with warm water and bandage	Second degree burns, on the other hand, do cause blistering of the skin and should be treated immediately. These burns should be immersed in warm water and then wrapped in a sterile dressing or bandage. (Do not apply butter or grease to these burns; despite the old wives' tale, butter does not help burns heal and actually increases the chances of infection.) If second degree burns cover a large part of the body, then the victim should be taken to the hospital immediately for medical care.
3rd degree: charred skin, hospitalize immediately	Third degree burns are those that char the skin and turn it black or burn so deeply that the skin shows white. These burns usually result from direct contact with flames and have a great chance of becoming infected. All third degree burn victims should receive immediate hospital care. Burns should not be immersed in water, and charred clothing should not be removed from the victim as it may also remove skin. If possible, a sterile dressing or bandage should be applied to burns before the victim is transported to the hospital.

This glossing is much more effective. For each paragraph, the sentences that express the main idea are trimmed down to the most essential words. In this way, the passage is boiled down to the key concepts in each paragraph: how each burn is different and how each burn gets treated.

Glossing provides a good quick reference for the main ideas of each paragraph. Because you're squeezing ideas into the margin—and because the whole point is to filter out the most important points—you don't have much room to indicate specific facts. You should limit your comments in the margin to the *general gist* of the paragraph. If you want to remember specific facts in a passage, then you should gloss *and* highlight or underline.

Why Glossing Works

Glossing is a strategy that benefits you in two ways. First, it forces you to identify the main idea of a paragraph. Second, it asks you to rewrite that main idea in your own words—in short form, since most topic sentences are too long to rewrite in the margin. Writing something down helps to seal it in your memory, and one of the most important things for you to remember is the main idea. In addition, once you've glossed a page, you can look down the margin and see how the main ideas of each paragraph work together to support the overall main idea of the passage.

PRACTICE 3

Go back to the passage entitled "A Bright, Bright Future" on page 82. Gloss each paragraph.

Answers

Your glosses in the margins might look something like these:

A Bright, Bright Future

demand for   **The demand for health care workers is on the rise.** The govern-

healthcare   ment's Bureau of Labor Statistics (BLS) reports that employment in

workers is   health service industries through the year 2005 **will grow at almost**

on the rise   **double the rate** of all other (non-farm) wage and salary employment. In sheer numbers, about 9 million American workers are now employed in health services. By 2005, that number is expected to be at about 13 million—**an increase of nearly 4 million jobs.**

job prospects   Within the allied health field in particular, prospects are looking

look good   good. Allied health embraces a wide range of careers—surgical technicians, dieticians, licensed practical nurses (LPNs), genetic counselors, and dental hygienists, to name a few. The fact is, employment in the vast majority of all allied health occupations is expected to increase at a much faster than average rate—at least 27 to 40 percent—through the year 2005.

primary cause of rise is managed care A primary factor contributing to the rosy outlook for allied health professionals is the "managed care" system taking root in the healthcare industry today. Health maintenance organizations (HMOs) offer a perfect example of managed care. HMOs operate by setting fixed fees for healthcare services provided under their plans. If those needs are met for less, that extra money becomes profitable for the HMO. In other words, the doctors don't decide what to charge for their services—the HMOs do. And oftentimes it simply costs less, without sacrificing quality care, to get an allied health professional to do certain things the doctor used to do.

doctors shifting focus; others handle pre/post care This doesn't mean doctors are going out of business. It means they're shifting their focus more toward the services only they are trained to do and leaving a broad range of services to other capable hands. Under managed care systems, more and more emphasis is being placed on pre-care and post-care which means placing more and more responsibility for healthcare delivery in the hands of allied health workers.

IN SHORT

By highlighting and underlining, you can mark the most important main and supporting ideas in a passage, as well as key words or definitions. By glossing a text, you can summarize the main idea of each paragraph in the margin. These strategies help you keep track of the key ideas conveyed in what you read.

Skill Building Until Next Time

1. Put these active reading strategies to use by highlighting, underlining, and glossing the things that you read throughout the week.
2. The next time you sit down to write—even if it's a personal letter to a friend—try glossing your paragraphs. This will help you practice finding the main idea and give you a notion of how you move from one idea to another.

CHAPTER | 9

Now that you're getting good at finding main and supporting ideas, you can begin to write effective notes and outlines. This chapter will show you how to make the most of these powerful comprehension and retention strategies.

TAKING NOTES AND OUTLINING

Taking notes and outlining are two effective ways to keep track of the important ideas and information conveyed in a text. They're quite similar strategies. The main difference is that outlines have a more formal structure than notes.

ASKING QUESTIONS AND TAKING NOTES

The secret to taking good notes is knowing what ideas and details are important. Therefore, a good way to set yourself up for taking notes is to ask the right questions.

Back in Chapter 1, you learned about pre-reading, in particular, about reading the *pre-text* and about *skimming ahead*. By skimming ahead, you can look for headings, main topics, and key words that can help you organize your notes or outline. First, any words that are defined in the text you're reading should probably be included in your notes. Second, you can use the pre-text and the various headings and divisions of a text to create questions that can guide you through the note-taking or outlining process.

For example, look back at Chapter 3 for a moment. The title and all of the main headings in the text of that chapter are listed below. Notice how the title and the first heading are used to form questions using the *who, what, where, when, why,* and *how* question words:

Using the Dictionary. How do you use one? When should you use one? Why should you use one?

Read the Entire Definition. When should you read the entire definition of a word? Why should you read the whole definition? How should you read it?

Use Context to Pick the Right Meaning
Parts of Speech
Special or Limited Definitions
How to Remember New Vocabulary

PRACTICE 1

Formulate questions for the remaining section headings listed above.

Answers

Answers will vary. Here are some questions you might have created:

Use Context to Pick the Right Meaning. When do you need to use context to pick the right meaning? How do you use the context to pick the right meaning?

Parts of Speech. What are parts of speech? Why do I need to know what they are? How can I tell them apart?

Special or Limited Definitions. What are special or limited definitions? How can you tell them apart from "regular" definitions?

How to Remember New Vocabulary. How can I remember new words? What tricks or strategies can I use?

KEYS TO TAKING GOOD NOTES

Good notes will answer many of your pre-reading questions. Specifically, good notes will:

1. Explain key terms
2. List main ideas
3. List *major* supporting ideas but not *minor* ones

For example, notes on the section in Chapter 3 entitled "Read the Entire Definition" might look something like this:

- Always read the whole definition
- Words often have more than one meaning
- Definition includes these three things:
    (1) phonetic spelling (how word is pronounced)
    (2) part of speech
    (3) meanings

PRACTICE 2

Write notes for any section of Chapter 3. Use your questions and the guidelines above.

Answer

Answers will vary because you will be putting some ideas into your own words. Here are possible notes for the topic *parts of speech:*

- Parts of speech describe the function of a word. There are four main parts of speech:
    1. A noun is a person, place, or thing (*beach*).
    2. A verb is an action (*shout*).
    3. An adjective describes a noun (*happy*).
    4. An adverb describes a verb, an adjective, or another adverb (*very, happily*).
- The meaning of a word depends upon its part of speech.
- Use context to determine a word's part of speech (how is it used in the sentence?)

Notice that these notes include the definition of each part of speech as well as one example.

PRACTICE 3

If you bought this book, that means you really want to improve your reading retention. So let's make the most of your money by helping you remember more of what you've read in this book. Remember, any time you write something down, you help to seal it in your memory. And any time you go back to an idea, you reinforce your memory and understanding of it.

Choose any part of any chapter so far (except Chapter 5) and take notes on it. Make sure it's a substantial part—at least a full page. For example, the following sample notes were taken from the first part of Chapter 6, "Finding the Main Idea." You should start by asking questions. Write your notes on a separate sheet of paper.

Answer

Your notes, of course, will depend upon what chapter and section you chose. Here are notes from Chapter 6. First is a list of questions one might ask from pre-reading. Then the notes for the section follow.

1. What is a main idea?
2. What is a topic sentence?
3. What are the characteristics of main ideas?
4. Where do I find topic sentences?
5. How are main ideas in paragraphs different from main ideas in essays?
6. How can main ideas help me remember what I read?

Here are the notes that answer the questions above:

1. The main idea is the overall fact, feeling, or thought the writer wants to convey about her subject.
2. Topic sentences are sentences that clearly express the main idea.
3. Main ideas:
   a. Say something about the subject
   b. Are general enough to be an "umbrella" for the passage
   c. Are assertions (claims that require evidence)

4. Topic sentences are often at the beginning of paragraphs, but they can be anywhere.
5. Main ideas of paragraphs work to support the overall main idea (thesis) of an essay.
6. Main ideas are the most important thing to remember.

OUTLINING

Outlining is very similar to note-taking. The main difference is that outlines are more structured than notes. That is, there's a certain way outlines should be organized. By organizing information the way they do, outlines help you remember ideas and information and see the relationships between those ideas. In an outline, you can see exactly which ideas each sentence supports.

The basic structure for an outline is this:

I. Topic
   A. Main idea
       1. Major supporting idea
           a. Minor supporting idea

Outlines can have many layers and many variations, but this is essentially how they work: you start with the topic, move to the main idea, add the major supporting idea, and then list minor supporting ideas (if they're important enough to write down).

A typical paragraph might be outlined like this:

I. Topic
   A. Main idea
       1. Major supporting idea
           a. Minor supporting idea
           b. Minor supporting idea
       2. Major supporting idea
           a. Minor supporting idea
           b. Minor supporting idea
       3. Major supporting idea
           a. Minor supporting idea
           b. Minor supporting idea

When you're working with a larger text, the overall main idea (thesis) should be at the top. Here's an example:

Ebonics controversy (topic)
I. Ebonics is more than just slang (thesis)
   A. Ebonics has distinct grammar patterns.
      a. Verbs are formed in a systematic way
        (1) The *s* is dropped in the third person ("He say")
      b. Use of "be" instead of "is"
        (1) For Example: "That be his car"
   B. Ebonics has its own pronunciation rules
      a. *sk* is pronounced *x*
      b. *th* is pronounced *f*

Outlining a text enables you to see the different layers of ideas and how these work together to support the overall main idea. When you outline, you do not have to include the minor supporting ideas, though you certainly may choose to do so.

PRACTICE 4

Outline part of any chapter you've completed so far. You might want to outline the section you had the most difficulty with. Outlining will help you remember and better understand the ideas in that chapter.

Answers

As usual, answers will vary. Here is an outline of Chapter 7:

I. Supporting ideas (topic)
A. Supporting ideas support a main idea like legs support a table (thesis)
   1. Main idea *tells*; supporting ideas *show*.
   2. Types of support include details, facts, statistics, etc.
   3. Distinguish main idea from support
      a. Signal words often introduce supporting ideas.
        (1) Examples: accordingly, also, as a result, furthermore, first of all, for example, etc.

(2) Signal words are *transitions:* words and phrases that signal a shift from one idea to the next.

   b. Ask two questions:

     (1) Is it general (main) or specific (support)?

     (2) Is there a transitional word that suggests it is a supporting idea?

4. Levels of support

   a. Main idea supported by major ideas

   b. Major ideas supported by minor ideas

IN SHORT

Taking notes and making outlines will help you to remember the important things in whatever you read. To take notes, write down the main idea and its major supporting ideas. By reading the pre-text and skimming ahead, you can create questions to guide your note-taking. You should also write down any key words defined in the text. Outlines have a more formal structure which show how ideas work together. In an outline, you can include major and minor supporting ideas.

Skill Building Until Next Time

1. Go back and take notes on or outline portions of each chapter you've completed so far.

2. Take notes on or outline portions of each chapter in the second half of this book.

CHAPTER | 10

This chapter pulls together
what you've learned in
Chapters 6–9 and gives
you more practice in
distinguishing main ideas
from major and minor
supporting ideas. You'll
also get to do more
underlining, highlighting,
glossing, note-taking,
and outlining as you
practice all the skills
you've learned so far.

PUTTING IT ALL TOGETHER

Congratulations—you've made it through half of the chapters in this book. To make sure you make the most of what you've learned, this chapter reviews Chapters 6–9 as well as strategies from Chapters 1–4.

IN BRIEF

Here are the reading skills that you learned in this section:

- **Chapter 6: Finding the Main Idea.** You learned that a main idea is the "umbrella" that holds together all of the ideas in a paragraph or passage. Main ideas are general assertions *about* the subject.

They're often expressed in topic sentences. In a larger text, there is an overall main idea—a thesis—supported by paragraphs with their own main ideas.

- **Chapter 7: Finding the Supporting Ideas.** You learned that writers use different kinds of details, facts, and examples to support their ideas. Supporting ideas are often indicated by transitional words and phrases. There are often several layers of support, and you learned how to distinguish between major and minor supporting ideas.
- **Chapter 8: Highlighting, Underlining, and Glossing.** You practiced highlighting and underlining the main ideas and major supporting ideas. You learned that it's important to be selective and that it's best to read through a text first and *then* highlight or underline. You also learned how to gloss by summarizing the main idea of each paragraph in the margin.
- **Chapter 9: Taking Notes and Outlining.** You learned how to take good notes by asking questions and then answering them. You also learned to outline to show the relationship between ideas—which ideas are major and which are minor.

If any of these terms or strategies sound unfamiliar to you, STOP. Take a few minutes to review the chapter or concept that is unclear.

PRACTICE 1

Begin your review by reading the following passage and answering the questions that follow. Use a separate sheet of paper.

The African country of the Democratic Republic of Congo has had a turbulent past. It was colonized by Belgium in the late 19th century. King Leopold officially declared it Belgian territory in 1895. The country, called the Belgian Congo after 1908, was under Belgian rule for 65 years. Then, in 1960, after several years of unrest, Congo was granted independence. The country was unstable for several years. Two presidents were elected and deposed, and there was much arguing over who should run the country and how. Finally, in 1965, a man named Mobutu Sese Seko rose to power. He changed the name of the country from Congo to Zaire.

Sese Seko was not a cruel dictator, but he certainly was rapacious. Zaire, which is rich in diamonds and other minerals, is one of the wealthiest African nations in terms of natural resources. Yet under Sese Seko's rule, the majority of Zairian people lived in complete squalor. They had no electricity, no running water, and no doctors, schools, or jobs to go to.

Finally, in 1997, after 32 years of growing poorer while their leader grew richer, the people of Zaire rebelled. Led by Laurent Kabila, rebels captured city after city with little bloodshed. As soon as his troops reached the capital, Kinshasa, Kabila changed the name of Zaire to the Democratic Republic of Congo.

1. Who are the three leaders of the Congo mentioned in this passage?
2. What names has the country had?
3. What does *rapacious* mean?
   a. violent
   b. lazy
   c. greedy
4. What does *squalor* mean?
   a. luxury
   b. poverty
   c. unhappiness
5. Highlight or underline the passage.
6. Gloss each paragraph.
7. What is the overall main idea of this passage?
8. Outline paragraph 2 to show major and minor support.

Answers

1. The three leaders mentioned in this passage are King Leopold, Mobutu Sese Seko, and Laurent Kabila.
2. The country has had these names: Democratic Republic of Congo, the Belgian Congo, and Zaire.
3. c. *Rapacious* means greedy.
4. b. *Squalor* means poverty.
5. Answers will vary. One way to highlight the passage is shown below (highlighted ideas are in bold).

6. Answers will vary. Here is one way to gloss the passage:

Congo—turbulent past

The African country of the Democratic Republic of Congo has had a turbulent past. It was colonized by Belgium in the late 19th century. **King Leopold** officially declared it Belgian territory in **1895.** The country, called the **Belgian Congo** after 1908, was under Belgian rule for **65 years.** Then, in **1960,** after several years of unrest, Congo was **granted independence.** The country was unstable for several years. Two presidents were elected and deposed, and there was much arguing over who should run the country and how. Finally, in **1965,** a man named **Mobutu Sese Seko rose to power.** He changed the name of the country from Congo to **Zaire.**

Sese Seko—greedy dictator

Sese Seko was not a cruel dictator, but he certainly was rapacious. Zaire, which is rich in diamonds and other minerals, is one of the wealthiest African nations in terms of natural resources. Yet under Sese Seko's rule, the majority of Zairian **people lived in complete squalor.** They had no electricity, no running water, and no doctors, schools, or jobs to go to.

People rebelled in 1997

Finally, in **1997, after 32 years** of growing poorer while their leader grew richer, **the people of Zaire rebelled.** Led by **Laurent Kabila,** rebels captured city after city with little bloodshed. As soon as his troops reached the capital, Kinshasa, Kabila changed the name of Zaire to the **Democratic Republic of Congo.**

7. The overall main idea of this passage is that the Congo has had a turbulent past.

8. Here is an outline of paragraph 2:

A. Main idea: Sese Seko was not cruel, but rapacious. (Supports *overall* main idea.)

   1. Zaire is one of the wealthiest African nations in terms of natural resources.

      a. Rich in diamonds

      b. Rich in minerals

2. Under Sese Seko's rule, most Zairian people lived in squalor.

    a. They had no electricity, running water, doctors, schools, or jobs.

If you missed	Then review
Question 1	Chapter 2
Question 2	Chapter 2
Question 3	Chapter 4
Question 4	Chapter 4
Question 5	Chapters 6, 7, and 8
Question 6	Chapters 6, 7, and 8
Question 7	Chapter 6
Question 8	Chapter 9

PRACTICE 2

For your second practice exercise, pre-read the following text to create questions for taking notes. Then, take notes on the passage.

Freud's Personality Theory

Sigmund Freud, the famous psychiatrist, made many contributions to the science of psychology. One of his greatest contributions was his theory of the personality. According to Freud, the human personality is made up of three parts: the id, the ego, and the superego.

The id is the part of the personality that exists only in the subconscious. According to Freud, the id has no direct contact with reality. It is the innermost core of our personality and operates according to the pleasure principle. That is, it seeks immediate gratification for its desires, regardless of external realities or consequences. It is not even aware that external realities or consequences exist.

The ego develops from the id and is the part of the personality in contact with the real world. The ego is conscious and therefore aims to satisfy the subconscious desires of the id as best it can within the individual's environment. When it can't satisfy those desires, it tries to control or suppress the id. The ego functions according to the reality principle.

The superego is the third and final part of the personality to develop. This is the part of the personality that contains our moral values and ideals, our notion of what's right and wrong. The superego gives us the "rules" that help the ego control the id. For example, a child wants a toy that belongs to another child (id). He checks his environment to see if it's possible to take that toy (ego). He can, and does. But then he remembers that it's wrong to take something that belongs to someone else (superego), and returns the toy to the other child.

Answers

Your questions and notes should look similar to what is written below. If not, review Chapter 9. You should also review Chapters 6 and 7.

Pre-Reading Questions
1. What is Freud's personality theory?
2. What is the id?
3. What is the pleasure principle?
4. What is the ego?
5. What functions according to the reality principle?
6. What is the superego?
7. What is an example of Freud's theory?

Notes

One of Sigmund Freud's greatest contributions was his **theory of personality.** According to Freud, the human personality is made up of the **id, ego**, and **superego.**

The **id** exists only in the subconscious. It operates according to the **pleasure principle**—it seeks immediate gratification for its desires. It's not aware of external realities or consequences.

The **ego** is conscious and aims to satisfy the id. When it can't satisfy the id, it tries to suppress it. It functions according to the **reality principle**.

The **superego** is the last part of the personality to develop. It contains our morals and values and helps the ego control the id. Example: Child wants toy (id), takes it (ego), remembers that it's wrong (superego), and returns it to the other child.

Skill Building Until Next Time

1. If you haven't had time to highlight, underline, gloss, take notes on, or outline Chapters 1–9, go back and do as many as you can now.
2. Write a paragraph about what you've learned since you picked up this book. Begin your paragraph with a clear topic sentence, such as "I've learned a lot about how to understand and remember what I read," and then support that topic sentence. Use both major and minor supporting details.

SECTION 3

IMPROVING YOUR READING IQ

In the first half of this book, you reviewed the fundamental reading skills and retention strategies that are essential for reading success. If you've been reading carefully and doing the practice exercises, you should already notice significant improvement in how much you understand and remember of what you read. Now it's time to take your skills to another level.

The chapters in this section are designed to help you improve your "reading IQ." They'll help you become more aware of the structure of what you read and show you active reading strategies that dramatically increase how much you understand and remember. Specifically, you'll learn how to:

- Recognize and anticipate different organizational patterns
- Tell the difference between facts and opinions
- Interact with the text to improve retention
- Remember more by visualizing what you read

CHAPTER | 11

Writers rely on a
few basic strategies
for organizing their ideas.
This chapter will show
you how to recognize
those common
organizational patterns
so you can better
understand what
you read.

RECOGNIZING ORGANIZATIONAL STRATEGIES

Remember "knock, knock" jokes? As different as the punchlines may be, they always follow the same pattern:

"Knock, knock."
"Who's there?"
"X."
"X who?"

And then the joke teller delivers the punchline. The beauty of these jokes is that they combine familiarity with surprise. When you hear a "knock, knock" joke, you know what to expect until the punchline.

You can have this kind of experience whenever you read, too. Once you learn to recognize common patterns of organization, you can anticipate the kind of information that will come next. The exact details will be a surprise, but once you see what kind of organizational strategy the writer is using, you can take a pretty good guess at what's ahead.

You already know that the underlying structure of most texts is *main idea* → *supporting idea*. But how do writers organize their support? This chapter covers eight common organizational strategies:

- general to specific
- specific to general
- chronological/sequential
- cause and effect
- spatial
- analysis/classification
- order of importance
- comparison and contrast

Like the *main idea* → *supporting idea* structure, these patterns work on both the paragraph level and on larger texts. An entire essay, for example, might be organized by comparison and contrast. Individual paragraphs in that essay, however, might use a variety of organizational patterns, including general to specific, cause and effect, and order of importance.

Now let's look at these eight organizational strategies and the transitions that can help you recognize them.

GENERAL TO SPECIFIC

Texts that follow this organization pattern begin with a *general* statement that is followed by several *specific* examples. Here's an example:

> More and more Americans are turning to alternative medicine. The ancient art of aromatherapy, for example, has gained a tremendous following, particularly on the West coast. Acupuncture, the traditional Chinese art of "needle

therapy," has doubled its number of active practitioners. And holistic medicine—treating the whole body instead of one part—is so popular that some HMOs now even pay for holistic care.

Whenever a paragraph begins with a general statement like the topic sentence above, it's often a sign that specific facts, details, or examples will follow. A statement like "more and more Americans are turning to alternative medicine" should make you want to know more specific information. What kind of alternative medicine? Why? A paragraph that answers the first question will use this general to specific format.

Sometimes writers make it easier to recognize this pattern by using the following transitional words and phrases to introduce their specific examples. These transitions include:

for example
for instance
in one case
specifically
in fact
in particular

PRACTICE 1

Read the sentences below carefully. Which sentences are general enough to make you anticipate specific examples will follow?

1. Adults now have more options for returning to school than ever before.
2. Pennies used to be made from real copper.
3. Candidates for political office experience a great deal of stress during their campaigns.

Answer

Sentences 1 and 3 are general enough to make you anticipate that specific examples will follow.

SPECIFIC TO GENERAL

As you might have guessed, this organizational pattern is the reverse of the general to specific pattern. Here, instead of starting with a general statement and following it with specific support, writers *start* with specific supporting ideas and *then* sum them up in a general statement. (In other words, this time, the topic sentence is at the end of the paragraph or text.) Here's an example you've seen before:

> When I was in kindergarten, I wanted to be an astronaut. When I was in junior high school, I wanted to be a doctor. When I was in high school, I wanted to be a teacher. Today, I'm 35 and I'm a firefighter. I had a lot of career goals when I was growing up, but none of them predicted what I'd actually turn out to be.

The first four sentences all provide specific examples of the main idea, expressed in the final sentence.

PRACTICE 2

Write a paragraph with a specific to general organizational pattern.

Answer

Answers will vary. Your paragraph is a good one if it begins with several specific points and ends with a general statement about those points.

CHRONOLOGICAL/SEQUENTIAL

With this pattern, ideas are presented in the order in which they did happen, should happen, or will happen. This kind of structure is usually easy to recognize and anticipate. There are a lot of signal words that writers use to help you keep track of time, including:

first, second, third	during	afterwards
then	after	since
next	while	until
later	when	now

Here's an example of a chronological/sequential paragraph. Notice how the paragraph describes the events in the order in which they happened and how the transitions *during* and *afterwards* show you this chronological order:

> The governor met today with leading education experts to discuss challenges in education for the next century. *During* the four-hour long talk, panel members discussed issues from city-wide standards to safety in schools. *Afterwards,* while the governor met with her cabinet members to draft a "Education Referendum," educators from the panel held a "town meeting" in Johnson Square.

PRACTICE 3

Below is a series of events listed in random order. Rewrite them in a paragraph organized by chronology. Use the transitional words and phrases in the sentences to determine the proper order.

- Once the investigation is complete, you will be ranked. 4
- If you pass the exam, you must then have an oral interview. 2
- In order to become a corrections officer in Texas, you must complete several steps.
- After your interview has been scored, your background will be investigated. 3
- Finally, after you are accepted, you must complete 120 hours of classroom instruction. 5
- First, you must take a written examination. 1

Answer

Here are the sentences in chronological order:

In order to become a corrections officer in Texas, you must complete several steps. First, you must take a written examination. If you pass the exam, you must then have an oral interview. After your interview has been scored, your background will be investigated. Once the investigation is complete, you will be ranked. Finally, after you are accepted, you must complete 120 hours of classroom instruction.

CAUSE AND EFFECT

When ideas are organized by cause and effect, they're arranged in one of the following two ways:

1. What happened (the cause) and what happened as a result (the effect)
2. What happened or will happen (the effect) and why it happened or will happen (the cause)

Certain types of sentences should lead you to expect a cause and effect organizational pattern. Here are some examples:

* There were many *factors that led up to* the Vietnam war. (You should expect *causes* to follow.)
* Turning farmland into housing developments *will have a negative impact* on our county's economy and ecology. (You should expect *effects* to follow.)
* When he decided to quit school, he had no idea *how that decision would change* his life. (You should expect *effects* to follow.)

The following transitional words and phrases help signal the cause and effect organizational pattern:

therefore	thus
because	consequently
as a result	accordingly
so	hence
since	then

PRACTICE 4

Write a brief paragraph using the cause and effect organizational pattern.

Answer

Answers will vary. Here's one possibility:

> The changes in the tuition reimbursement policy will have several negative effects. Employees will be less loyal to the

company. They will also be less likely to seek opportunities to increase their knowledge. In addition, they will be less likely to advance within the company, so management positions will have to be filled from outside rather than inside when there are vacancies.

SPATIAL

In some texts, ideas are organized according to spatial principles: from top to bottom, side to side, inside to outside, and so on. Transitional words showing that a text is spatially organized include:

beside	beyond
next to	behind
around	in front of
above	under
below	near

PRACTICE 5

Read the following paragraph carefully. What is the specific spatial principle the writer has used to organize her ideas? What transitional words help you follow her organization?

The human body is covered by a "suit of armor"—the skin. The skin offers three layers of protection. The outer most layer is called the keratin. This is what we see when we look at skin. Beneath the keratin is the epidermis. Nerve cells are located in the next level, the dermis. And underneath these three layers is the subcutaneous tissue, which contains the sweat glands.

Answer

The paragraph is organized from outside to inside, or top to bottom. The transitional phrases are *beneath, in the next level,* and *underneath.*

ANALYSIS/CLASSIFICATION

In texts arranged by analysis or classification, ideas are organized according to the *parts, functions,* or *types* of something. The text you read about the different kinds of burns was one example of this structure. Here's another:

The model 6017A fax machine has several important functions. First, it is, of course, capable of sending and receiving faxes. Second, it can print documents directly from your PC. Third, it can copy documents.

Sometimes analysis/classification calls for transitional words you've seen before, like *first, second, third*. The biggest clue to the analysis or classification type of organization is any sentence with the following pattern:

- "X has several parts."
- "There are three types of X."
- "X has several different functions."
- "X is made of four different components."

PRACTICE 6

In the following paragraph, underline the sentence that leads you to expect an analysis/classification pattern of organization, and then circle words or phrases that signal the classes or parts that the writer divides his subject into.

There are three types of readers. The unskilled reader is easily distracted and thinks of reading as a passive task. This reader doesn't make any effort to understand or remember what she reads. The skill-building reader knows that reading is an active task but is still learning how to make the most of active reading strategies. Finally, the skilled reader reads actively and responds to what she reads.

Answer

<u>There are three types of readers</u>. The (unskilled reader) is easily distracted and thinks of reading as a passive task. This reader doesn't make any effort to understand or remember what she reads. The (skill-building reader) knows that reading is an active task but is still learning how to make the most of active reading strategies. Finally, the (skilled reader) reads actively and responds to what she reads.

ORDER OF IMPORTANCE

With this pattern, ideas are presented in order of *most* important to *least* important or vice versa—from *least* important to *most* important. Several key transitional words and phrases often guide readers through this kind of organization:

more importantly	furthermore	first, second, third
moreover	above all	first and foremost
in addition	certainlyl	ast but not least

The passage about burns in Chapter 8 is not only organized by classification/analysis; it's also organized by order of importance. It starts by describing the least serious burn (1st degree) and ends with the most serious burn (3rd degree). Here are examples of the type of sentences that set up this kind of organization:

- There are three reasons you shouldn't vote for Ms. Roberts. First of all . . .
- Studies show there are important health benefits of eating fresh broccoli. One benefit is . . .

PRACTICE 7

Read the following paragraph carefully. Is it organized from most to least important or least to most important? How can you tell?

It is essential that young adults begin to build a solid credit rating as soon as they are of age. First of all, a good credit rating makes it much easier to acquire credit cards, which are important for further building your credit. Second, a good credit rating is essential for getting a loan or mortgage. Third, if you are ever in a serious emergency, your good credit rating will make it possible for you to get the money, credit, or assistance you need because you've proven that you're trustworthy.

Answer

This paragraph is organized from least to most important. Because the third reason deals with emergencies, it is the most important.

COMPARISON AND CONTRAST

When writers want to show how two or more things are similar and/or different, they arrange their ideas in a comparison and contrast format. Comparisons show *similarities* while contrasts show *differences*.

There are two ways writers organize comparison and contrast texts. For example, let's say a writer wants to compare his previous job (Job A) with his current job (Job B). There are three different characteristics of A and B that he wants to compare: (1) the compensation, (2) the job duties, and (3) the job environment.

If this writer were to use the **block technique**, he would deal with each job individually. That is, he would discuss each of these three characteristics for Job A and then each characteristic for Job B. The structure of such a passage would look like this:

First paragraph

Job A1—compensation

Job A2—duties

Job A3—environment

Second paragraph

JobB1—compensation

Job B2—duties

Job B3—environment

If this writer were to use the **point-by-point technique**, on the other hand, he would be making a more direct comparison. In a point-by-point comparison and contrast, writers organize ideas by *characteristic* rather than by *item*. Thus, the writer would compare compensation for both jobs first, then duties at both jobs, then finally the environment in both companies.

First paragraph

Job A1—compensation

JobB1—compensation

Second paragraph

Job A2—duties

Job B2—duties

Third paragraph

Job A3—environment

Job B3—environment

A number of transitions signal the comparison and contrast organizational structure:

Words to signal comparison:

likewise

similarly

like

in the same way

also

Words to signal contrast:

on the other hand	yet	although
however	nevertheless	nonetheless
on the contrary	rather	despite
unlike	instead	in contrast
but	whereas	conversely

PRACTICE 8

Here's an example of a comparison and contrast paragraph. Which organizational method does it use?

> *Darwinism vs. Creationism.* Both Darwinism and Creationism are theories that explain the origin of life on earth. Creationists believe that humans and all living beings on the Earth were created by God. Darwinists, on the other hand, maintain that living creatures came about as a result of evolution—that is, today's life forms evolved from earlier, simpler life forms. Creationism is a theory based in religion, whereas Darwinism has its roots in scientific investigation.

Answer

This paragraph uses the point-by-point technique.

Multiple Strategies

It's important to remember that many texts use two or more organizational strategies at the same time. For example, the paragraph below uses both the cause and effect and order of importance patterns:

> Too much sun can be deadly. First of all, too much sun can dry your skin, which in turn reduces its elasticity and speeds the aging process. Second, too much sun can burn unprotected skin and cause permanent discoloration and damage the dermis. Most importantly, long-term exposure of unprotected skin can result in skin cancer.

Meanwhile, this individual paragraph, which combines two different organizational strategies, may be part of a larger text that is organized by a different strategy, such as analysis/classification. And the various paragraphs within that text may use different strategies and combinations of strategies. The point is that both on the "big picture" level (the entire text) and on the level of individual paragraphs, organizational patterns are at work. If you can recognize them, you can anticipate what's ahead, and this makes it easier to receive that information. In addition, it's much easier to remember things that are in patterns. The more you recognize patterns in what you read, the easier it will be to remember that information.

PRACTICE 9

Read each sentence below carefully. Based on the sentence, what kind of information do you expect to follow? What organizational pattern will the writer use?

1. The shape and size of a widget depends upon what it will be used for.
2. A hesitating engine may be the sign of several different problems.
3. A union meeting was held on Thursday, May 8, at 8 a.m.
4. Euthanasia is a highly controversial issue.
5. There are many differences between ice cream and frozen yogurt.

Answers

1. I expect to learn what kinds of things widgets are used for. Analysis/classification pattern.
2. I expect to learn what might cause an engine to hesitate. Cause and effect pattern.
3. I expect to learn what happened at the meeting. Chronological/sequential pattern.
4. I expect to know exactly why euthanasia is a controversial issue. General to specific pattern.
5. I expect to learn about the differences between ice cream and frozen yogurt. Compare and contrast pattern.

IN SHORT

Writers use different patterns to organize their ideas. These organizational patterns include:

- General to Specific
- Specific to General
- Chronological/Sequential
- Cause and Effect
- Spatial
- Analysis/Classification
- Order of Importance
- Comparison and Contrast

Writers often use certain transitional words and phrases to signal their organizational pattern. By recognizing a writer's organizational pattern, you can anticipate what's ahead and better remember what you read.

Skill Building Until Next Time

1. Try to determine the organizational pattern of the things you read today and throughout the week. Remember that writers can use more than one strategy at a time.
2. Practice asking "anticipation" questions. Whenever you come across signal words or sentences that suggest a certain structure, ask questions about what's next.

CHAPTER | 12

One of the most
important signs of a
good reader is the ability
to distinguish between
fact and *opinion*. This
chapter will show you
how facts are different
from opinions and how
this distinction can help
you remember more.

DISTINGUISHING FACT FROM OPINION

"**J**ust the facts, ma'am, just the facts." This often-quoted line comes from the 1960s television series "Dragnet." On the show, Detective Joe Friday and his partner would solve crimes by piecing together the facts of each case. When Detective Friday told a witness that he was looking for "just the facts," he was making an important distinction between *fact* and *opinion*. It didn't matter to him who witnesses *thought* did it or what witnesses *thought* happened. Rather, he needed to know what *really* happened.

The key difference between fact and opinion lies in the difference between *believing* and *knowing*. Opinions may be based on facts, but

What are Facts?

- Facts are things *known* for certain to have happened.
- Facts are things *known* for certain to be true.
- Facts are things *known* for certain to exist.

they are still what people think or believe, not what they know. Opinions are debatable; facts are not. For example, "Basketball is the most exciting sport" is debatable; you might disagree. Thus, it's an opinion. But "Basketball is a team sport" is not debatable; it's impossible to disagree with this statement. It's a fact; it's known for certain to be true.

You will understand and remember more if you can distinguish between fact and opinion—between what the writer *thinks* and what the writer *knows*, between what is proven to be true and what needs to be proven. This is largely because you can react to an idea once you identify it as either a fact or an opinion. You'll learn more about this in Chapter 13.

ASKING QUESTIONS

A good test for whether something is a fact or opinion is to ask yourself, "Can this statement be debated? Is this known for certain to be true?" If

What are Opinions?

- Opinions are things *believed* or *thought* to have happened.
- Opinions are things *believed* or *thought* to be true.
- Opinions are things *believed* or *thought* to exist.

you can answer yes to the first question, you probably have an opinion. If you can answer yes to the second, you probably have a fact. For example, think back to the topic sentences you created in Chapter 6. Were they assertions that expressed fact, or opinion? Here's one topic sentence from that chapter:

The number of work-related accidents has dropped by 50 percent.

Does this topic sentence express a fact or an opinion? Well, is it debatable? Can someone disagree? Probably not. It's a matter of fact; something proven to be true by the specific statistics provided in the rest of the paragraph.

Now look at this topic sentence:

Vanessa is a wonderful supervisor.

Is this idea debatable? Definitely. Someone else might think she's a lousy supervisor, and someone else might think she's just okay. This sentence is clearly a matter of opinion.

PRACTICE 1

Determine whether the following sentences are *fact* or *opinion*:
1. America is a democratic country.
2. America must preserve democracy at all costs.
3. The meetings should be held on Tuesdays, not Wednesdays.
4. These meetings are held Wednesdays.
5. These meetings are often a waste of time.

Answers
1. Fact
2. Opinion
3. Opinion
4. Fact
5. Opinion

WHEN FACTS AND OPINIONS ARE MIXED TOGETHER

It's usually easy to determine whether something is fact or opinion when it's standing alone like the sentences you just reviewed. It's a little more complicated when you're working with paragraphs and larger texts. That's because unless what you're reading is a textbook or a scientific or technical manual, you'll probably come across a *combination* of facts and opinions, sometimes even in the same sentence. Here's an example:

> Email and other technologies make it possible for many people to work from home, and companies should fully support employees who want to "telecommute."

The first part of the sentence expresses a fact; technology has indeed made telecommuting possible for a lot of employees. But the second part of the sentence—that companies should support the folks who want to work from home—is clearly debatable. It is an opinion.

PRACTICE 2

Here's a paragraph that has both fact and opinion. See if you can correctly identify which ideas are debatable and which are not. Underline the facts and use a highlighter or colored pen to highlight the opinions. (Some things may be neither; just leave those sections as is.)

New York and other U.S. cities have begun using vehicles powered by natural gas. This is a good idea, because vehicles that use natural gas do not pollute the air. Pollution is the biggest problem facing cities right now. Furthermore, natural gas is more cost-effective than regular gas. All cities should use only vehicles powered by natural gas.

Answer

New York and other U.S. cities have begun using vehicles powered by natural gas. **This is a good idea,** because vehicles that use natural gas do not pollute the air. **Pollution is the biggest problem facing cities right now.** Furthermore, natural gas is more cost-effective than regular gas. **All cities should use only vehicles powered by natural gas.**

SUPPORT FOR OPINIONS

Because facts are things that are known to be true, readers generally don't need *evidence* that they're true. Readers *do* want details, explanations, or examples, but they often don't need you to prove your case.

Opinions, on the other hand, are debatable, and they always need evidence. Readers need to see *why* writers think and say what they do. Often this evidence will come in the form of facts. But just because a writer offers evidence for an opinion doesn't mean readers have to agree with that opinion. The same facts can often be used to support many different opinions.

Still, an opinion that is supported by evidence (examples, details, reasons, explanations, or statistics) is much stronger than opinions that stand alone. For example, read the two paragraphs below. In one, the writer supports her opinion, but in the other she does not.

Edward Wilson was an outstanding employee and a great supervisor. He was a nice guy, too.

Edward Wilson was an outstanding employee. He came to us as an entry-level production worker and worked so well with others that he became a team leader within a year. He was such an excellent team leader that the following year he was promoted to supervisor. While he was a supervisor, his crew consistently met or exceeded production goals and had the fewest problems of any team with quality control. In addition, Edward was a very kind and generous person. He often went out of his way to help the people he supervised. He covered their shifts in emergencies, gave them rides home when they worked overtime, and helped them resolve conflicts with others.

Why is the second paragraph so much better than the first? Because the second paragraph offers you more than just opinions. It offers opinions supported by specific facts and examples. The first paragraph, on the other hand, is just opinions. Every sentence is debatable. Every sentence says what the author *thinks* is true, but not what is *known* to be true.

The author of the first paragraph doesn't provide any evidence to support why she thinks Edward Wilson was a great employee. As a result, we're not likely to take her opinion very seriously—certainly not as seriously as we take the opinion of the writer of the second paragraph.

PRACTICE 3

To strengthen your ability to distinguish between fact and opinion, try this exercise. Take a fact, such as:

Many companies have dress down days on Fridays.

Then turn it into an opinion. Make a debatable statement about the same subject, like the following:

1. Dress down days improve employee morale.
2. Every day should be a dress down day.

3. Dress down days make workers less productive.

4. Dress down days make workers more productive.

Write three facts in the space below. Then, turn each fact into an opinion. Make sure your facts are not debatable, and make sure your opinions are. In fact, you may want to write two opposing opinions just to make sure that your opinions are debatable (like 3 and 4 above).

1.

2.

3.

Answers

Answers will vary depending upon what facts you chose. Here are a few examples of facts turned into opposing opinions:

Fact: Wednesdays are in the middle of the week.
Opinions: Wednesdays are always the longest day of the week.
             Wednesdays are the most exciting day of the week.

Fact: Next Tuesday is election day.
Opinions: Everyone should vote in next Tuesday's election.
             No one should bother voting in next Tuesday's election.

Fact: Reading to your children when they're very young will help
             them do better in school.
Opinions: All parents should read to their young children every day.
             Parents should not read to their children.

HOW DISTINGUISHING BETWEEN FACT AND OPINION CAN HELP YOU REMEMBER

Distinguishing between fact and opinion can help you remember more of what you read because it helps you think critically about what you read. When you're distinguishing between fact and opinion, you're essentially asking yourself, "Is this something I should accept as true?" You can also determine how you feel about an issue that the writer offers an opinion about. You'll see more about this in Chapter 13.

IN SHORT

Facts are things *known* for certain to be true. *Opinions*, on the other hand, are things *believed* to be true. To distinguish between fact and opinion, determine whether the idea is *debatable* or not. If it is debatable, it's an opinion. Good writers will support their opinions with evidence: details, examples, facts, and so on.

Skill Building Until Next Time

1. Listen carefully to what other people around you say today. Are they stating facts or expressing opinions? When they offer opinions, do they provide support for them? Is it enough support for you to find their opinion convincing?
2. Read the editorials in your newspaper this week. Notice how good editorial writers use specific facts and examples to support their opinions.

CHAPTER | 13

One of the most effective active reading strategies is to "talk back" to the writer. By recording your questions and reactions in the margin or on a piece of paper, you can create a dialogue that helps you better remember what you read.

RECORDING YOUR QUESTIONS AND REACTIONS

When you read, you usually don't have the opportunity to speak with the author, to ask questions and make comments about the material. But that doesn't mean you can't say what's on your mind. In fact, if you *do* say what's on your mind, you're much more likely to remember what you read. That's because you are both *interacting with* and *reacting to* the text, responding to the ideas and information the author provides.

This kind of active reading takes several forms. Most reader reactions fall into these main categories:

- Asking questions
- Agreeing and disagreeing
- Making connections
- Evaluating

ASKING QUESTIONS

You've already studied how to ask questions to help you anticipate what's ahead. The kinds of questions discussed here are questions you ask *in response to* the ideas you read. Is there anything you don't understand? Something you want to know more about? Below is an example of how this kind of questioning works. Read the following paragraph carefully and notice the questions in the margin:

No-Smoking Policy

How many smokers are there? ratio of smokers vs. non-smokers?

Could company sponsor programs to help smokers quit?

What p[ro]blems w[ould] it solve

Could t[hey] make a[ ]smoki[ng] lounge

    Instituting a no-smoking policy in the office would create more problems than it would solve. First of all, employees who smoke would be forced to leave the building in order to smoke. That means they would have to take longer breaks, and, as a result, they'd spend less time working. They'd also have to take fewer breaks so that their breaks can be longer. That means there'll be longer stretches of time between cigarette breaks. Consequently, these employees will be more irritable. Furthermore, we risk losing employees who are long-term smokers. These employees may very well quit to find another company that will let them smoke while they work.

    Asking questions like these shows you're thinking critically about what you read. In addition, because you're formulating questions in response to the ideas in the text, you're more likely to remember those ideas. And asking questions encourages you to find the answers to those questions.

AGREEING AND DISAGREEING

You're also much more likely to remember what you read if you know how you feel about the ideas a writer conveys. When a writer offers an opinion, you don't have to simply accept or reject it. You can—and should—*react* to it. Do you agree or disagree with it? Do you think what the writer said is brilliant, or malarkey? Why?

Here's the no-smoking policy paragraph again, this time with a reader's reactions in the margins.

e to be of sec- hand ke

Instituting a no-smoking policy in the office would create more problems than it would solve. First of all, employees who smoke would be forced to leave the building in order to smoke. That means they would have to take longer breaks, *Not necessarily* and, as a result, they'd spend less time working. They'd also have to take fewer breaks so that their breaks can be longer. That means there'll be longer stretches of time between ciga- *only if they're* rette breaks. Consequently, these employees will be more irri- *seriously addicted* table. Furthermore, we risk losing employees who are long-term smokers. These employees may very well quit to find *or it just might help* another company that will let them smoke while they work. *"light" smokers quit smoking*

might be good for them

Reacting to a writer's ideas forces you to slow down a bit, and that's a good thing—you can focus on ideas longer and make sure you understand them. In addition, reacting to ideas helps you make a connection to your own feelings, which in turn helps lock the ideas in your memory. After all, think of it this way: If you meet a bunch of people at a party, who do you still remember a month later? You're most likely to remember those people with whom you either agreed or disagreed passionately.

PRACTICE 1

Read the following passage carefully and actively. As you read, record your questions and reactions in the margins.

Imagine how wonderful it would be if you had a four-day work week. Rather than working five eight-hour days (40 hours), you'd work four ten-hour days (still 40 hours). Then, you'd have Friday, Saturday, and Sunday off. This would give you a three-day weekend *every week*. The benefits of this extra day would be numerous. You'd have a full day for running errands that you can't get done while you're at work; a day to clean while your kids are at school so that you could have leisurely family weekends; one less day of child care expenses you'd have to pay; an extra day for you to rest. Psychologically, you would also benefit by feeling that there's almost a fair balance in your life between work (four days) and rest (three days).

Answer

this would be great!

wouldn't you still have to pay for at least 40 hours of child care?

what about people who already work a 10-hour day?

this is important

Imagine how wonderful it would be if you had a four-day work week. Rather than working five eight-hour days (40 hours), you'd work four ten-hour days (still 40 hours). Then, you'd have Friday, Saturday, and Sunday off. This would give you a three-day weekend every week. The benefits of this extra day would be numerous. You'd have a full day for running errands that you can't get done while you're at work; a day to clean while your kids are at school so that you could have leisurely family weekends; one less day of child care expenses you'd have to pay; an extra day for you to rest. Psychologically, you would also benefit by feeling that there's almost a *fair balance* in your life between work (four days) and rest (three days).

MAKING CONNECTIONS

You can also help yourself remember what you read by making connections. You can make connections between:

1. Different ideas within the text
2. The text and your own experience

For example, look at how the reader makes connections as she reacts to the passage below: Her "connections" are on the left, and her questions are on the right.

ABC Chemical of Williamsburg, Ohio, is in hot water. Local environmentalists discovered last week that the company's plant has been leaking toxic chemicals into the town's water supply.

Not another leak!

County records indicate that there has been a large increase in stomach ailments and short-term memory loss in the area.

How many residents have been affected?

The company spokesperson, Mel Gerardi, insists that ABC Chemical executives knew nothing of the leak. According to Gerardi, the company passed the city's Environmental Commission inspection just last month. How the leak went undetected, he says, is a mystery.

Sounds suspicious to me

Could there be a cover-up?

Local residents have threatened ABC Chemical with a class-action suit for negligence.

I'd sue them too

A similar case is pending in Richdale, Arkansas, where a pesticide company was found to have been emitting toxic fumes into the neighborhood. For several weeks, residents had complained of stomach pain and general nausea as well as difficulty remembering things. The cause was eventually traced back to the pesticide plant.

John lives in Richdale

People in both towns had similar sicknesses

What toxins are responsible?

How are companies supposed to dispose of them?

Making Connections to Remember More

Making connections between different ideas in the text will help you remember those ideas. Reacting to an idea is like tying it down with one string in your brain. But one string is easily broken. If you take notes, you add another string, and it's more likely you'll remember that idea. If you make a connection between that idea and another idea in the text, you add another string. And if you make a connection between the text and your own experience, you add yet another string. Every time you review the material, you tie it down with yet another string, so that soon the information is thoroughly anchored in your memory.

Making connections between the text and your own experience also makes the ideas and information that you learn more practical and real.

If you can put to use the ideas or information that you read, you're more apt to remember it.

EVALUATING

After improving your ability to think actively and critically about what you read, you can begin *evaluating* what you read. This means asking yourself questions like the following:

- Does the writer provide *enough evidence* to support his or her ideas?
- Does the writer provide *strong support* for his or her ideas?
- Are the writer's ideas organized?

Here's an example of how you might evaluate the paragraph below. You've seen this paragraph before. Read it again carefully.

> Edward Wilson was an outstanding employee and a great supervisor. He was a nice guy, too.

Now take a look at how a reader evaluated this paragraph:

- What made him such a good employee? The writer doesn't give me any details or evidence.
- What made him a great supervisor?
- How do I know he was a nice guy?
- Was the writer a good friend of Edward? Can I trust his opinion?

These questions and comments show that the reader is really thinking about what she's reading. The more she thinks about it, the more effective use she can make of the material, and the easier it will be for her to remember it.

PRACTICE 2

Read the following paragraph carefully. Then, write some comments that evaluate the paragraph.

Talk shows like "Rikki Lake" and "Jerry Springer" should be banned from network television. Too many people get hurt, both physically and emotionally. Besides, who wants to see other people airing their dirty laundry?

Answers

You might have written comments like the following in the margin or at the end of the paragraph:

1. The paragraph doesn't include any specific examples of people getting hurt, either physically or emotionally.
2. To ask that these shows should be banned is a pretty strong request. This kind of statement should have lots of support.
3. Obviously, *lots* of people want "to see other people airing their dirty laundry"—these shows consistently have high ratings. It seems this author just doesn't like these shows and is trying to pass his opinion off on others.

PRACTICE 3

Now it's your turn to combine all of the kinds of comments and questions discussed in this chapter. Read the following passage carefully and record your questions and reactions in the margins. Be sure to include some evaluation of the passage.

Safety in the Workplace

The United States Postal Service has a reputation as a dangerous place to work. There have been a few cases in recent years of disgruntled postal workers attacking fellow employees and their supervisors. But the United States Postal Service is actually one of the country's safest places to work.

Construction work, on the other hand, is the most dangerous. Yearly accident rates at construction sites across the country are high. Many of these accidents are fatal.

Many workplace accidents happen because employees fail to follow standard safety procedures. Ladder falls are among the most common workplace accidents.

Answers

Answers will vary, of course, depending upon your knowledge and past experience. Here's one reader's reaction to the passage:

Safety in the Workplace

For a while I was afraid to go! — The post office has a reputation as a dangerous place to work. There have been a few cases in recent years of disgruntled postal workers attacking fellow employees and their supervisors. But the United States Postal Service is actually one of the country's safest places to work.

I'd like to se some statistics.

Attack is an understatement—people have been <u>killed</u>.

I disagree

Construction work, on the other hand, is the most dangerous. Yearly accident rates at construction sites across the country are high. Many of these accidents are fatal.

Again, I'd li to see som statistics

Many workplace accidents happen because employees fail to follow standard safety procedures. Ladder falls are among the most common workplace accidents.

That's how Sue got hu

There is a difference between job that require physical risi a construct worker) and that don't (post office clerk). So, is a fair comparision

IN SHORT

Recording your questions and reactions as you read will help you remember more. When you read something, you should write the following in the margin:

- Your questions
- Your reactions to the writer's ideas and opinions
- Connections you make to other parts of the text or to your own experience
- Your evaluation of the text, particularly how well (or how poorly) the writer provides support

Skill Building Until Next Time

1. Record your questions and reactions for everything you read throughout the week (even the Sunday paper!).
2. Notice how you respond when someone is telling you ideas or information either over the phone or face to face. What kind of questions do you ask? Do you agree or disagree? What connections do you make? How do you evaluate what the speaker is saying?

CHAPTER | 14

Sometimes the details and
descriptions you read
may seem overwhelming,
but you can use them
to your advantage.
By paying close
attention to descriptive
words and details,
you can create a vivid,
memorable picture
in your mind's eye.

VISUALIZING TO REMEMBER

Picture this: you're alone on a soft, white beach. The crystal-clear water is 80 degrees—just the right temperature. You're relaxing in a hammock strung between two mango trees. A gentle breeze keeps you cool as you soak up the sun. The soft, slapping sound of the waves caressing the beach slowly lulls you to sleep. . . .

Did you see yourself there on the beach just now? Were you able to picture it just for a moment? The mind's ability to create pictures is a very powerful tool, and you can use this tool to help you remember what you read.

HOW TO VISUALIZE

Back in kindergarten, the books you "read" were filled mostly with pictures, not words. Now most of what you read is made up only of words. Because humans are very visually oriented, we tend to remember much better when we can *see* things as well as hear or read them. So learning to picture what you read can be a great asset. There are two steps to visualizing what you read:

1. Pay attention to actions.
2. Pay attention to description and details.

Pay Attention to Actions

Carefully follow the *action* in the text you're reading. Who is doing what, and how? Then, picture that "who" actually performing those actions in the way that the text describes. (If there's no specific "who," picture *yourself* in that role.)

Let's bring back a passage that you've seen before as an example. Read it carefully, paying particular attention to the actions. There's no clear "who" in this passage, so picture yourself as the "employee." Imagine yourself experiencing each of the consequences described for employees who test positive:

A new mandatory drug testing policy will take effect at our Detroit office on July 1. Under this new policy, all employees will be required to take a urine test four times throughout the year. These tests will be unannounced. Employees who refuse to take the tests will be automatically suspended without pay.

An employee who tests positive for substance abuse will face several consequences. To start, the employee will be immediately suspended without pay. In addition, the employee must issue a statement explaining how he tested positive for illegal substances. Then, a 3-member employee panel will be assigned to review the employee's case. A "typical" violator might be permitted to return to work on probationary status and be required to attend counseling.

The new drug testing policy may seem strict, but it is designed to improve the health and safety of all employees of Data Management Co. Indeed, our attempt to create a drug-free workplace is modeled after the programs that have improved overall workplace safety for other companies around the country. Furthermore, we feel that a drug-free workplace will improve employee morale while it reduces sick days and down time.

As part of the policy, we have added a counselor to our staff. Dr. Jennifer Jenkins has extensive experience as a work-place counselor, particularly in dealing with substance abuse. Her office is located next to Denise Robinson's in Human Resources.

If you read this text and picture yourself going through these actions, you're much more likely to remember the policy—especially because it's not a situation you'd ever like to see yourself in. By visualizing, you make an "action movie," so to speak, of the text, and that makes it come alive. Now you not only have the words but a picture to match them as well.

Pay Attention to Description and Detail

By paying attention to description and detail, you can create a clear picture of the people, places, and things you read about. Of course, some texts will be very short on description and detail. In that case, there's not much you can do. But writers will often offer descriptions and details like the following:

size	time	type/kind
shape	location	material
color	texture	origin/source
style	sound	name
design/pattern	smell	age
temperature	brand name	gender
date	taste	

Practice 1

Look around the room and write down as many details and descriptions as you can, using the list above as a guide. For example, you might write: "The rug is light brown. It has a coffee stain here by the wall." Try to write at least a dozen observations, and try to be as specific as possible. For example, don't just say "book"—give the title. Don't just write "red"—describe the exact shade. Crimson? Scarlet? Brick red?

Answers

Answers will vary, of course. You should have a wide range of details and descriptions, the more specific the better. Here's a sample response:

1. My desk is a long rectangle, about 4 feet long, 2 feet wide and 2 and a half feet tall.
2. My desk is made of maple and is stained a dark brown, the color of cola.
3. There is a stack of magazines—*Newsweek, Sports Illustrated, National Geographic and Gourmet*—about a foot high on my desk.
4. There is an old tin coffee mug filled with #2 pencils on my desk.
5. Next to the mug is a pile of half-completed crossword puzzles ripped out of *The New York Times.*
6. There is a large yellow stain on the varnish of my desk in the top left corner, the size and shape of an angle fish.
7. The floor is covered by a hunter green rug, slightly shaggy, very worn.
8. A big dust ball is stuck between the back right leg of my desk and the wall.
9. The wall is a soft off-white.
10. The ceiling is a shade lighter than the wall.
11. The ceiling has a long, thin crack running from one corner, zig-zagging slightly to just about the middle of the ceiling, where the light is hanging.
12. The paint is just beginning to peel right around the light fixture.

VISUALIZING THROUGH COMPARISONS

Writers know how important it is for readers to be able to "see" what they read. That's why they often make comparisons that help create a picture for their readers. "He was angry as a tornado" is an example. This compares someone's anger to the fury of a tornado. This kind of comparison creates a clear picture in your mind, so you can *see* how angry this person is.

You probably come across and even use comparisons like this all the time. Here are a few of the most common:

> He slept like a log.
> She's pretty as a picture.
> He cried like a baby.
> It was fast as lightning.

Beyond these common comparisons, you'll find more unusual (and therefore more effective) ones like the following:

> She sat in her office like a bird in a cage.

This kind of comparison is meant to create a certain picture in your mind. Imagine how a bird sits in a cage. Now, imagine how a person might sit if she were sitting in her office in a similar way. Based on this comparison, which of the following statements do you think is true?

a. She loves to be in her office.
b. She feels trapped in her office.
c. She has a bird at home.

The answer is **b**—she feels trapped, just like a bird is trapped in a cage.

Here are more examples. Read the comparisons carefully and let them create vivid pictures in your mind.

> The curtains fluttered in the wind like butterflies.
> The employees marched in like soldiers.
> Amy slouched in her chair like a limp dishrag.

Authors of these comparisons (also called *similes*) don't mean to say, for example, that Amy *actually* looks like a limp dishrag. These aren't literal comparisons. But her posture *reminds* the writer of a limp dishrag. By comparing her to a dishrag, the writer has created a picture for readers of a woman who is sitting hunched over, crumpled up, worn out. With this comparison, readers can *see* just how she slouches.

PRACTICE 2

Below is an excerpt from the beginning of Booker T. Washington's autobiography, *A Slave Among Slaves*. The ellipses (. . .) indicate that some of the text has been cut out. Notice how descriptive Washington's narrative is. As you read, underline all of the descriptive words and details you see and try to create a vivid picture in your mind's eye of the cabin where Washington lived.

I was born a slave on a plantation in Franklin County, Virginia. I am not quite sure of the exact place or exact date of my birth, but at any rate I suspect I must have been born somewhere and at some time. As nearly as I have been able to learn, I was born near a cross-roads post–office called Hale's Ford, and the year was 1858 or 1859. . . .

My life had its beginning in the midst of the most miserable, desolate, and discouraging surroundings. This was so, however, not because my owners were especially cruel, for they were not, as compared with many others. I was born in a typical log cabin, about fourteen by sixteen feet square. In this cabin I lived with my mother and a brother and sister till after the Civil War, when we were all declared free. . . .

The cabin was not only our living-place, but was also used as the kitchen for the plantation. My mother was the plantation cook. The cabin was without glass windows; it had only openings in the side which let in the light, and also the cold, chilly air of winter. There was a door to the cabin—that is something that was called a door—but the uncertain hinges by which it was hung, and the large cracks in it, to say nothing of the fact that it was too small, made the room a very uncomfortable one. In addition to these openings there was, in the lower right-hand corner of the room, the "cat-hole." . . . The "cat-hole" was a square opening, about seven by eight inches, provided for the purpose of letting the cat pass in and out of the house at will during the night. . . . There was no wooden floor in our cabin, the naked earth being used as a floor. In the centre of the earthen floor there was a large, deep opening covered with boards, which was used as a place in which to store sweet potatoes during the winter.

Answer

I was born a slave on a plantation in <u>Franklin County, Virginia</u>. I am not quite sure of the exact place or exact date of my birth, but at any rate I suspect I must have been born somewhere and at some time. As nearly as I have been able to learn, I was born <u>near a cross-roads post-office</u> called <u>Hale's Ford</u>, and the year was <u>1858 or 1859</u>. . . .

My life had its beginning in the midst of the most <u>miserable</u>, <u>desolate</u>, and <u>discouraging</u> surroundings. This was so, however, not because my owners were especially cruel, for they were not, as compared with many others. I was born in a typical <u>log cabin</u>, about <u>fourteen by sixteen feet square</u>. In this cabin I lived <u>with my mother and a brother and sister till after the Civil War</u>, when we were all declared free. . . .

The cabin was not only our living-place, but was also used as the kitchen for the plantation. My mother was the plantation cook. The cabin was <u>without glass windows</u>; it had only <u>openings in the side</u> which let in the light, and also the <u>cold</u>, <u>chilly</u> air of winter. There was a door to the cabin—that is something that was called a door—but the <u>uncertain hinges</u> by which it was hung, and the <u>large cracks</u> in it, to say nothing of the fact that it was <u>too small</u>, made the room a very <u>uncomfortable</u> one. In addition to these openings there was, in the <u>lower right-hand corner of the room</u>, the "<u>cat-hole</u>." . . . The "cat-hole" was a <u>square</u> opening, about <u>seven by eight inches,</u> provided for the purpose of letting the cat pass in and out of the house at will <u>during the night</u>. . . . There was <u>no wooden floor</u> in our cabin, the <u>naked earth</u> being used as a floor. In the centre of the earthen floor there was a <u>large, deep opening cov-</u><u>ered with boards</u>, which was used as a place in which to store <u>sweet potatoes during the winter</u>.

DRAW YOUR OWN PICTURES

When you come across technical or spatial descriptions (like the layout of a room, for example), you can visualize what you read in another way: on paper. Use the description the writer provides to draw what is being described. Don't worry—you don't have to be an artist to draw a sketch that can help seal information in your memory.

For example, imagine that you're interested in architecture and you're reading a book about classical Greek columns. The book describes the columns but doesn't show you any pictures. Based on the descriptions in the following paragraph, you might try to draw each column.

There are three types of Greek columns. What makes them different is the tops, or capitals. *Doric* columns have the simplest capitals. The bottom of the capital takes a short, sharp turn in. Then it completes a half circle and turns back out beyond the column to curve up in the shape of a large, flat bowl. *Ionic* columns have more ornate capitals. Where the Doric capital curves in and then out, Ionic capitals remain straight and are decorated with leaf-like swirls and patterns. Laying on top of this section is a large scroll-like section. The two rolls of the scroll lay on either side of the capital. *Corinthian* columns are the most elaborate of the Greek columns. Whereas the other types have two distinct layers in their capitals, here, the capital is one piece decorated with several layers of swirling, scrolling leaves and floral designs. The layers are shaped so that the capital resembles an upside-down bell.

PRACTICE 3

Reread the passage above and draw pictures of the Ionic and Corinthian columns. Here is a sample drawing for the first type of column, Doric.

Doric

Answer

Here are sample drawings of the other two types of columns:

Ionic   Corinthian

Creating a picture—whether it's in your mind's eye, on paper, or both—will help you remember what you read.

PRACTICE 4

As a final practice exercise, read the following passage. Pay attention to both actions and details and try to picture who does what and how. Create a "movie" in your mind's eye. Then, answer the questions that follow. They're designed to see how well you paid attention to action and detail. If you do this well, you shouldn't have to look back at the passage to answer the questions. After you complete the exercise, turn to the end of this chapter to see if the diagram of the accident matches the view in your mind.

Yesterday, May 12, at 8:15 a.m., I was walking to work when I witnessed an accident. I was walking east down Elmont Avenue—right in front of the main entrance to the college, to be exact—when I saw a red 1997 Corvette speeding west on the avenue, heading toward the intersection of Woodrow Street, about 100 yards in front of me. At the same time, a black Nissan Sentra approached the same intersection from the north on Woodrow Street. I guess the driver of the Nissan didn't see the Corvette because he pulled out into the intersection. Maybe it was the sun glare—it was pretty bright that morning. A moment later, the cars collided. The front of the Corvette crunched up like an accordion and the Nissan, which was hit in the front, spun around like a top. I immediately ran into the college to call for help. The police and an ambulance both arrived by 8:20 a.m. Fortunately, no one was seriously hurt.

1. When did the accident happen?
2. Where was the witness when the accident happened?
3. Which car was speeding?
4. What color was each car?
5. How far was the witness from the accident?
6. What might have caused the accident?
7. What happened to each car?
8. How long did it take for help to arrive?

Answers

1. The accident occurred at 8:15 a.m.
2. The witness was on Elmont Avenue, right in front of the college.
3. The Corvettte was speeding
4. The Corvette was red and the Nissan was black.
5. The witness was about 100 yards away.
6. Sun glare might have caused the accident.
7. The front of the Corvette was crunched like an accordion and the Nissan spun around like a top.
8. It took only 5 minutes for help to arrive.

IN SHORT

Creating a picture—either in your mind, on paper, or both—can help you remember what you read. Pay attention to actions and to descriptions and details as well as to comparisons. Put yourself in the place of the person who is performing the action to make it more real. By creating an "action movie" in your mind, you bring the reading material to life and strengthen its place in your memory. You can also draw a diagram of the material.

Skill Building Until Next Time

1. As you go throughout your day, pay attention to details. What color is the chair you're sitting in, for example? What pattern is the fabric? What is the chair made of? What condition is it in? What kind of shoes is the person next to you wearing? What size? Color? Brand? Condition? The more you are able to notice the world around you, the easier it will be to pick up details and description in what you read. And that will help you to visualize and remember what you read.

2. Whatever you write this week, add some specific details and action words. Try to add a vivid comparison, too.

Accident Diagram

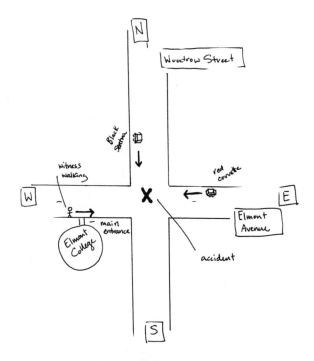

CHAPTER | 15

This chapter pulls together what you learned in Chapters 11–14 as well as strategies from the first half of the book. You'll review how to recognize organizational strategies, distinguish fact from opinion, record questions and reactions, and use visualization to improve retention.

PUTTING IT ALL TOGETHER

You've learned a lot in this section about ways to improve your "reading IQ." Before putting all of these strategies together in some practice passages, let's take a minute to review the last four chapters.

IN BRIEF

This is what you learned in this section:

- **Chapter 11: Recognizing Organizational Strategies.** You learned how to recognize common patterns that writers use to organize ideas and information. Writers use general to specific, cause and effect, order of importance, chronology, comparison and contrast, and other patterns of organization. You learned that most texts use many different organizational strategies throughout though they have one main strategy overall. You also learned to ask questions to anticipate what's next.

- **Chapter 12: Distinguishing Fact from Opinion.** You practiced distinguishing what is *known* to be true from what is *believed* to be true. You also looked at how writers use facts and other evidence to support their opinions.
- **Chapter 13: Recording Your Questions and Reactions.** You learned several strategies for active and critical reading. You learned to ask questions about the ideas and information in the text and to agree or disagree with the writer whenever he offers an opinion. You also learned to make connections both within the text and between the text and your own life and to evaluate the text for its support and other issues.
- **Chapter 14: Visualizing to Remember.** You practiced looking for actions, descriptions, and details (like color, size, shape, pattern, and so on) so that you could create a memorable picture of what you read. You also learned to make the most of vivid comparisons and practiced actually drawing pictures based on descriptions you read.

If any of these terms or strategies sound unfamiliar to you, STOP. Take a few minutes to review the chapter or concept that is unclear.

PRACTICE 1

Read the following paragraph carefully and actively. Then answer the questions that follow.

The damage from the fire is significant. The lobby, where the fire started, is completely charred. It's as black as a tar pit. None of the furniture or fixtures are salvageable. The chairs are nothing but piles of black ashes. The lobby will have to be completely rebuilt. The accounting office to the left of the lobby is also badly burned. Three of the four desks are unusable and all of the electronic equipment but the fax machine is ruined. Two of the walls are burned through in places. To the right of the lobby, the Human Resources office suffered no fire damage (except for the door) but significant smoke and water damage. There's a thin layer of ashy slime on the floor and a layer of soot covers everything in the office like a blanket.

1. Where did the fire begin?
2. Outline the paragraph to show the main idea and major and minor support.
3. How is this paragraph organized?
4. Underline any opinions.
5. Identify two vivid comparisons.

Answers

1. The fire began in the lobby.
2. Here is an outline of the paragraph:
   A. *Main idea:* The damage from the fire is significant.
      (1.) *Major support:* The lobby is completely charred.
         a. *Minor support:* It's black as a tar pit.
         b. *Minor support:* None of the furniture or fixtures are salvageable.
      (2.) *Major support:* The accounting office is also badly burned.
         a. *Minor support:* Three of the four desks are unusable
         b. *Minor support:* All of the electronic equipment but the fax machine is ruined.
         c. *Minor support:* Two of the walls are burned through in places.
      (3.) *Major support:* The Human Resources Office suffered significant smoke and water damage.
         a. *Minor support:* There's a thin layer of ashy slime on the floor.
         b. *Minor support:* A layer of soot covers everything in the office like a blanket.
3. This paragraph is organized spatially and in order of importance (most damage to least damage).
4. There aren't many opinions in this passage. The only ideas that are debatable are those that comment on the degree of the damage, specifically: "The damage from the fire is significant," "The accounting office

to the left of the lobby is also badly burned," "The lobby will have to be completely rebuilt," and the Human Resources office suffered "significant smoke and water damage."

5. Two vivid comparisons are "black as a tar pit" and "a layer of soot covers everything in the office like a blanket."

If you missed	Then review
Question 1	Chapter 2
Question 2	Chapters 6, 7, and 8
Question 3	Chapter 11
Question 4	Chapter 12
Question 5	Chapter 14

PRACTICE 2

Here's your second practice passage. First, skim through it quickly and then answer the pre-reading questions. Don't use a dictionary. Then, read the passage carefully and answer the questions that follow on a separate piece of paper.

Pre-Reading Questions:

1. List the two main topics in the passage.
2. Based on these topics, write several questions that you expect the passage to answer.

Commit to Recycling

Recycling programs only work if the members of the community are committed to the recycling effort. To be committed, people need to believe that what they're doing is important or right. If they don't believe that their part matters—that recycling the can of soda they just drank can make a difference—they won't do it.

Recycling is Right

It's not only right to recycle; it's our *duty* to recycle. In the natural world, every thing is recycled. A dead animal, for example, becomes food for many levels in the food chain, down to organisms in the soil. Nothing is wasted. But humans, who have created so many materials that can't be broken down by nature, create permanent litter that kills animals and pollutes water and soil. If nature can't reuse it, we *must* recycle it. It comes down to a simple rule we learned in kindergarten: whoever makes a mess must clean it up.

Recycling is also the right thing to do because we consume resources at a much faster rate than our earth is able to replenish them. The earth is rich in resources, but its supply of materials is not endless. Recycling can help us reduce the risk of depleting our natural resources.

Recycling is also right because it's good for our pocket books. Products made from recycled materials cost less than those made from raw materials. A ream of recycled paper, for example, costs less than regular manufactured paper—and it doesn't kill any trees.

Post-Reading Questions:

3. What does *deplete* (paragraph 3) mean?

    a. use up

    b. make use of

    c. reverse

4. Gloss this passage.

5. What is the overall main idea of the passage?

6. How are paragraphs 2–4 organized?

7. Underline or highlight any opinions in the passage.

8. Write responses to these opinions.

9. Make at least one connection between the passage and your personal experiences.

10. Evaluate this passage. Do you feel the author provides sufficient support? Why or why not?

Answers

1. The two main topics are "commitment to recycling" and "recycling is right."
2. You might have asked questions like: Why should we commit to recycling? What is involved in this commitment? Why is recycling right?
3. **a.** *Deplete* means to use up.
4. Here's what you might write in the margins next to each paragraph:
   Paragraph 1: recycling programs need commitment
   Paragraph 2: it's our duty to recycle.
   Paragraph 3: recycle because we consume resources faster than we replenish
   Paragraph 4: recycling is good for our pocket books
5. The main idea is that recycling is important and right. This idea is mentioned in every paragraph.
6. Paragraphs 2–4 are organized by most to least important.
7. Here's the passage with the opinions in boldface:

> *Commit to Recycling*
> **Recycling programs only work if the members of the community are committed to the recycling effort. To be committed, people need to believe that what they're doing is important or right. If they don't believe that their part matters—that recycling the can of soda they just drank can make a difference—they won't do it.**
>
> *Recycling is Right*
> **It's not only right to recycle; it's our *duty* to recycle.** In the natural world, every thing is recycled. A dead animal, for example, becomes food for many levels in the food chain, down to organisms in the soil. Nothing is wasted. But humans, who have created so many materials that can't be broken down by nature, create permanent litter that kills animals and pollutes water and soil. **If nature can't reuse it, we *must* recycle it. It comes down to a simple rule we learned in kindergarten: whoever makes a mess must clean it up.**
> **Recycling is also the right thing to do** because we consume resources at a much faster rate than our earth is able to

replenish them. The earth is rich in resources, but its supply of materials is not endless. Recycling can help us reduce the risk of depleting our natural resources.

Recycling is also right because it's good for our pocket books. Products made from recycled materials cost less than those made from raw materials. A ream of recycled paper, for example, costs less than regular manufactured paper—and it doesn't kill any trees.

8. You might have written something like: "People also recycle because they'll get fined if they don't" or "Children should learn about the importance of recycling in school."

9. You might have written something like: "I should make an effort to buy recycled products" or "My coworkers could do a much better job of recycling."

10. The author could provide more specific support, especially in the last paragraph. How much cheaper is a ream of recycled paper, for example?

If you missed	Then review
Question 1	Chapter 1
Question 2	Chapter 1
Question 3	Chapter 4
Question 4	Chapter 9
Question 5	Chapter 6
Question 6	Chapter 11
Question 7	Chapter 12
Question 8	Chapter 13
Question 9	Chapter 13
Question 10	Chapter 13

Skill Building Until Next Time

1. Review the Skill Building activities from this section. Try any Skill Builders you didn't do or didn't complete.
2. This weekend, read something that you enjoy (such as a novel). As you read, be sure to respond and visualize. Especially if it's a novel, you'll have plenty of vivid description and details to create pictures in your mind.

SECTION 4

READER, DETECTIVE, WRITER

As you can see by now, successful readers employ many different strategies at once. They also take on many different roles. That is, to be a good reader, you also need to be a bit of a detective and writer.

In this section, you'll learn how to be a "detective" and to look for clues that help you determine meaning. You'll also find out how to rewrite what you read so you can better remember it. Specifically, you'll learn:

- How a writer's word choice, point of view, and tone affect meaning
- How to find an implied main idea
- How to summarize and paraphrase a text

Each of these strategies will help you understand and remember more.

CHAPTER | 16

Writers can convey meaning in both direct and indirect ways. One way that they can create meaning is through their choice of words. This chapter shows you how even a small change in word choice can make a big difference in meaning.

WORD CHOICE AND POINT OF VIEW

What made Sherlock Holmes such a genius at solving crimes? Was he just so much smarter than everyone else? Was he somehow able to see into the future or into the past? No, Sherlock Holmes didn't have any magical powers. He simply made the most of a power that all of us have: the power of *observation*.

In Chapter 14, you began using your powers of observation to notice details and descriptive language. You looked carefully at the practice passages and noticed specific things about *how they were written*. This helped you create a vivid picture of the people, places, and actions in the text. By noticing the specific words writers use to describe, define, inform, and explain, you can also make important *inferences* about how those writers feel about their subject.

MAKING INFERENCES

Inferences are conclusions based on reason, fact, or evidence. For example, if you see that the sky is black and you hear thunder, you can infer (come to the conclusion) that it's going to rain. Good observations lead to good inferences, which can help you determine meaning, just as they helped Sherlock Holmes solve crimes.

What's an Inference?
An *inference* is a conclusion based on reason, fact, or evidence.

To become a better reader, then, you need to be more like Sherlock Holmes: you need to be more observant. In the story "The Adventure of the Blanched Soldier," Sherlock Holmes tells a client, "*I see no more than you, but I have trained myself to notice what I see.*" You don't have to be Sherlock Holmes to be a good reader. You just have to train yourself to notice what you see.

MAKING OBSERVATIONS ABOUT WORD CHOICE

The same idea can be conveyed in many different ways, and the words a writer chooses to convey that idea can greatly affect its meaning.

For example, look at the three sentences below. They all convey essentially the same information, but because of their choice of words, the actual message of each sentence is quite different:

A. This is a risky situation.
B. This is a dangerous situation.
C. This is an explosive situation.

What do you notice about these three sentences? How are they different? All three sentences show that the situation is uncertain and potentially harmful. But notice the difference in the three words used to describe the situation. One describes the situation as *risky*; another as *dangerous*; and another as *explosive*. Based on the writers' *diction* or word choice, which writer seems to be the *least* worried about the situation? Which one seems to be the *most* worried?

The writer of the first sentence appears to be the least worried, since *risky* is less serious than either *dangerous* or *explosive*. *Dangerous* is serious, but *explosive* is probably the most serious. In an explosive situation, things could erupt at any moment and cause incredible destruction (even if there aren't any explosives involved). Thus, the writer of the last sentence is the most worried about the situation.

> **What's Diction?**
> *Diction* refers to the specific words writers choose to convey their message.

By using different words to characterize the same situation, each writer actually communicates a unique message that reveals how he feels about the situation.

DENOTATION AND CONNOTATION

There are many different ways to say *dangerous*. In fact, in the English language, there are many different ways to say most things. Think for a moment of all the different ways you can say "I'm tired":

I'm exhausted.	I'm worn out.
I'm sleepy.	I'm beat.
I'm weary.	I'm wiped out.

If you looked each of these words up in a dictionary, you'd see that they all have similar definitions. But in reality, none of them mean exactly the same thing. That's because in addition to their dictionary definitions (called *denotation*), words also have a level of meaning called *connotation*. Connotation is the meaning that is implied or suggested by the word. It is the social or emotional impact that the word carries.

> **What's Denotation?**
> *Denotation* is a word's dictionary definition.

For example, *tired*, *sleepy*, and *weary* all mean the same thing—the dictionary definition for *tired* is often *sleepy* or *weary*, and vice versa. Yet these three words have different connotations—different degrees of meaning. *Sleepy* is the gentlest of the three. If you're sleepy, a nap would be nice, but you're not going to drop from exhaustion. *Tired* is a word that requires more rest—say, a full night's sleep. And if you're *weary*, you might need to stay

> **What's Connotation?**
> Connotation is a word's implied or suggested meaning.

in bed for the whole weekend. *Weary* also suggests an emotional tired-
ness that *tired* and *sleepy* do not.

PRACTICE 1

Two sets of words with essentially the same meaning are listed below. If
you're not familiar with these words, look them up in the dictionary.
Then, rank them according to their strength from weakest or least serious to the strongest or most powerful word.

1. **a.** dive
    b. fall
    c. plummet
    d. tumble

2. **a.** deceive
    b. fib
    c. lie

Answer

Here are the words ranked from least serious to most serious:

1. **d.** tumble
    b. fall
    a. dive
    c. plummet

2. **b.** fib
    c. lie
    a. deceive

HOW WORD CHOICE INFLUENCES MEANING

A writer's word choice doesn't just *affect* meaning: it *creates* it. Word
choice shows how the writer feels about her subject. It also shows something about the writer's relationship to the reader. For example, notice
what the difference in word choice in the following sentences reveals.
Both sentences *say* the same thing (they provide the same information),
but they say it in two very different ways:

A. We need to get together to hammer out a new schedule.

B. We need to meet to arrange a new schedule.

Sentence A uses the words *get together* and *hammer out* while the other, sentence B, uses the words *meet* and *arrange*. Now, what inference or conclusion can you come to based on this difference in word choice?

a. Writer A has a more formal relationship with the reader than Writer B.

b. Writer B has a more formal relationship with the reader than Writer A.

c. Both writers have the same kind of relationship with the reader.

Answer **b** is correct. Even if you know nothing about these writers or readers, you can safely *infer* from the diction of the two sentences that Writer B has a more formal relationship with the reader than Writer A. That's because *meet* is a more formal word than the phrase *get together*, and *arrange* is more formal than *hammer out*.

PRACTICE 2

Read the following pairs of sentences carefully. On a separate sheet of paper, write down your observations. What do you notice about the word choice in the sentences? Then, answer the inference questions that follow.

Group A

A. Union representatives said that negotiations with management were at a complete standstill.

B. Management said that talks with union representatives were stalled at the moment.

Inference questions:

1. Which party (the union or management) presents a more positive view of the negotiations? How can you tell?

2. Which sentence presents the more serious situation? How can you tell?

Group B

A. Rhonda has a very colorful way of speaking.

B. Rhonda has a very showy way of speaking.

Inference question:

3. Which sentence is more critical of Rhonda? How can you tell?

Answers

1. The management presents a more positive outlook. You can tell because sentence B uses the word *talks* instead of *negotiations*. In addition, sentence B uses the word *stalled*, whereas union representatives use the word *standstill* in sentence A. *Stalled* suggests a temporary stop rather than a complete stop. The temporary nature of the stall is emphasized by the phrase *at the moment*.

2. The union representatives present the more serious situation. See #1.

3. Sentence B is more critical of Rhonda. The word *showy* suggests that she's too colorful.

RECOGNIZING POINT OF VIEW

Point of view is the person or perspective through which the writer channels her information and ideas. Just as you may look at a physical object from a number of different perspectives (from above it, below it, behind it, beside it, and so on), you can look at information and ideas from different perspectives as well (yours, his, hers, the company's, the union's, the employee's, and so on).

> ### Point of View
> *Point of view* is the person or perspective through which the writer channels his information and ideas.

All of these perspectives, however, fall into two main categories: that of the insider (someone directly involved in the action) and that of the outsider (someone not directly involved in the action).

For example, remember the accident at Elmont Avenue and Woodrow Street discussed in Chapter 14? The writer's account is that of an insider—not because the witness was *in* the accident but because the witness *saw* the accident. The police officer who writes the report of the accident, on the other hand, has an outsider's perspective, since she was not involved and was not a witness.

When it comes to expressing point of view, writers can use three distinct approaches:

- First person point of view
- Second person point of view
- Third person point of view

First Person Point of View

In the first person point of view, the writer or narrator uses the pronouns *I, me, mine, we, our* and *us* to express a highly individualized, personal point of view. In other words, writers are talking about themselves and their own thoughts, feelings, and experiences. And they're sharing these thoughts, feelings and experiences directly with the reader. Here's an example:

> As a firefighter, *I* work hard to save lives and protect people's property.

This point of view creates a certain level of intimacy or closeness between reader and writer. It also means you have to keep in mind that the writer is *subjective*. That is, because the writer is presenting things from his own point of view, his personal experiences, desires, and motives directly influence how he feels about the subject. Both the drivers in the Elmont Avenue accident and the witness would describe the accident from this point of view.

Second Person Point of View

In the second person point of view, the writer uses the pronoun *you* to speak directly to the reader. Often, the effect is that the writer puts the reader in his own shoes. For example, notice how the sentence below changes when you replace the first person *I* with the second person *you*. Suddenly, the reader is put in the position of the firefighter:

> As a firefighter, *you* work hard to save lives and protect people's property.

As a result, it's hard not to imagine, if only for a moment, what it might be like to be a firefighter.

Third Person Point of View

In the third person point of view, the writer or narrator removes herself and presents a *third person*. The writer uses the pronouns *he, him, his; she, her, hers; it, its;* and *they, them, theirs*. This point of view creates a certain distance and objectivity because the thoughts are not expressed as the *writer's* personal thoughts. With the third person point of view, there's no direct person-to-person relationship between writer and reader, even if the writer still addresses the reader as "you."

For example, notice the difference between the following sentences:

> Sentence A: We wish you well in your retirement, Joe.
>
> Sentence B: The company wishes you well in your retirement.

In Sentence A, the first person *we* speaks directly to the reader, *you*. In Sentence B, on the other hand, the good wishes are sent by a "third person," the company.

Because the third person point of view is (or at least appears to be) objective, it's the point of view the police officer reporting on the accident at Elmont Avenue would probably use in her report.

Here's the firefighter sentence again, this time using the third person point of view:

> As a firefighter, *one* must work hard to save lives and protect people's property.
>
> *Firefighters* work hard to save lives and protect people's property.
>
> *They* work hard to save lives and protect people's property.

NOTE: Be careful. Writers can express very subjective (personal) opinions in the third person to make them *seem* objective.

Here is a table that summarizes the three different points of view and their effects:

Point of View	Pronouns	Effects
1st person	I, me, mine, we, our, us	Intimacy between the writer and reader. Suggests objectivity; based on the experience of the speaker or writer
2nd person	You	Puts the reader in the writer's shoes.
3rd person	He, him, his; she, her, hers; it, its; they, them, theirs.	Creates distance between the writer and reader. Suggests objectivity; not influenced by the thoughts and feelings of the writer.

DRAWING CONCLUSIONS BASED ON POINT OF VIEW

The point of view writers use can help you to make inferences about how they feel about their subjects. For example, look again at the two sentences referring directly to the reader:

A. We wish you well in your retirement, Joe.
B. The company wishes you well in your retirement.

If you were Joe, which message would you rather receive? Most people would probably prefer to receive memo A. Why? What's the difference between these two messages? They both say the same thing, don't they?

Point of view, like word choice, helps create the meaning of a message. The writers of both memo A and memo B address the reader as "you." But you probably also noticed that the writers chose two different points of view to refer *to themselves*. Memo A uses the first person "we" (and addresses the reader directly as "Joe") whereas memo B uses the third person ("the company") to refer to the sender. As a result, memo A seems more sincere; it comes *from* a person *to* a person, rather than from "the company" (a thing) to a person.

What does this tell you? From the point of view, what can you tell about the attitude of these memo writers toward their subject (Joe)? Writer B, by using the third person point of view, suggests that there is— and that he'd like to keep—a distance between the reader and the writer. Writer A, on the other hand, doesn't mind the person-to-person "contact" created by the first person point of view.

Memo B sends the unwritten message, "Let's not get too close or personal—let's keep our distance." Memo A, on the other hand, uses the first person to say, "We're real people here at the head office. We acknowledge you as a person and you can acknowledge us as people, too." Thus, point of view reflects the way the senders wish to be perceived (as a distant thing or a friendly person). Word choice also shows you how the senders perceive their subjects. Memo A acknowledges the reader as a real person with a name whereas in Memo B, the reader is an employee who remains nameless.

PRACTICE 3

Read the sentences below and answer the questions that follow.

Sentence A: I think our new office policy is a failure.
Sentence B: The new office policy appears to be a failure.

1. Which point of view does Sentence A use?
   a. first person
   b. second person
   c. third person
2. Which point of view does Sentence B use?
   a. first person
   b. second person
   c. third person
3. Which sentence do you think is more effective in the following situations? Why?
   a. Submitting a complaint to office management.
   b. Informally complaining to a co-worker.

Answers

1. Sentence A uses **a**, the first person point of view.

2. Sentence B uses **c**, the third person point of view.

3. **a.** In this situation, Sentence B would be more effective because someone from the outside (a third person, not the reader or writer) is judging the policy. The third person point of view is almost always considered to be more objective because the third person is not directly involved in the action. The first person *I*, however, *is* directly involved in the action (the policy) and therefore cannot have a truly objective opinion about the policy's success or failure. That doesn't mean, however, that a first-person opinion is necessarily less valid or that a third person point of view is always objective. It just *appears* that way. You'll have to think critically about the specific situation to decide how much weight the opinion carries.

   b. In such an informal situation, Sentence A would certainly be appropriate and more effective.

HOW WORD CHOICE AND POINT OF VIEW HELP YOU REMEMBER

By being more aware of the words and point of view writers choose to convey their ideas, you'll be able to understand much more of what you read. And when you understand more, you can remember more. As you build your observation skills and your understanding of the way words work on different levels, you'll be more aware of language. Then you'll be able to remember ideas more easily and accurately.

IN SHORT

Looking carefully at a writer's word choice can help you determine how the writer feels about her subject. Because words have both a denotation and a connotation, they can *suggest* meaning indirectly. Point of view is the perspective the writer uses to refer both to herself and to the reader. The first person point of view creates intimacy between the reader and writer, the second person point of view addresses the reader directly, and the third person point of view suggests objectivity and distance.

Skill Building Until Next Time

1. Think about the words you choose when you speak to people. Do you use different types of words for different people? Do you think carefully about what you say and which words you will use? How aware are you of your own diction?

2. Notice how much the meaning of a sentence can change when a single word is altered. Form a simple sentence, like: "Eating junk food will make you sick." Now, replace *sick* with synonyms that have slightly different meanings and connotations, like *unhealthy, feeble, ill, dying,* and *under the weather.* Each word will express a slightly different attitude about your subject to the reader. Insert synonyms into your sentence and see how much the meaning is altered. Choose words like *rich, happy,* or *sad* that have many synonyms with a wide range of connotations.

CHAPTER | 17

Your ability to determine *tone* can determine whether or not you understand what a writer is trying to say. This chapter shows you how to analyze word choice and point of view to "hear" the tone of a written text.

DETERMINING TONE

S ay this word out loud: "Sure."

How did you say it? Did you say it with a smile, as in "Sure, any time"? Or did you say it flatly, as if responding to a command? Or did you stretch the word out, "*Suuuure,*" as if you didn't believe what someone just said to you? Or did you ask it, as in, "Are you *sure* this is okay?"

Perhaps you didn't realize there were so many ways to say this one word, "sure." But there are. Why? The word itself doesn't change, so there can't be any change in denotation or connotation. So how can the same word express so many different things?

The difference in the meaning of all of these *sures* comes from the *tone*. How you *say* the word determines what you mean by it and how your listeners will feel when they hear you say it. Your tone of voice conveys your message.

When you speak and listen, you can hear the tone of your own and the other's voice. You know what someone means when he says "sure." But how do you determine tone in writing when you can't actually hear the writer's voice? How do you know whether to whisper "sure" or shout it out loud? Fortunately, tone, like the meaning of unfamiliar words, can be determined from context.

What's Tone?

Tone is the mood or attitude conveyed by words or speech.

Think about how tone is created in speech. When you say "sure," your tone changes according to how loudly or softly you say the word and how slowly or quickly you say it. Tone is also conveyed by a speaker's expressions and body language. In writing, of course, you do not have these auditory and visual clues. But you do have plenty of written clues to help you determine tone. These clues come both from the writer's word choice (diction) and the point of view.

HOW POINT OF VIEW AND WORD CHOICE CREATE TONE

It may help you to think of a sentence as a collection of ingredients (words and phrases) that result in a dish (an idea). Word choice and point of view are like the spices you use to give your dish a certain flavor. Different spices will result in different flavors or different *tones*. And tone, in turn, helps reveal how the writer feels about her subject.

For example, look at the two letters below. Both convey essentially the same information. But they have two rather different tones, and therefore they have two different effects on the reader. Pay particular attention to word choice and point of view to see how these different tones are created.

A. Thank you for your request. A catalog has been sent to your address. It should arrive shortly. Your interest is appreciated.

B. Thank you for requesting our catalog. You should receive a copy in a few days. We look forward to your business.

Which of these letters has a more positive tone? Which one has a more positive effect on the reader? Why? What do you notice about Letter B that is different from Letter A?

Perhaps you notice that Letter B uses key words like "look forward," "your business," "for you," and "in a few days." Letter B also uses the first person point of view to represent its writers. It's *our* catalog, not *a* catalog; *we* put it in the mail and *we* look forward to your business. Letter B is warmer, friendlier, more human, and more likely to get the reader's business than the distant, unfriendly Letter A.

VARIETIES OF TONE

Just as there are endless varieties of tone of voice, there are also endless varieties of tone in writing. Here's a list of some of the more common words used to describe a writer's tone:

apologetic	foreboding	insecure
authoritative	gloomy	insincere
bored	hopeful	ironic
cheerful	humorous	playful
complementary	angry	sad
critical	bitter	sarcastic
demanding	urgent	sincere
disrespectful	indifferent	threatening
hesitant	forceful	reluctant
eager	excited	enthusiastic
suspicious	skeptical	

If any of these terms are unfamiliar to you, look them up in a dictionary right now. You may need them in the following exercise.

PRACTICE 1

Look at the sentences below to see if you can correctly identify their tone. As you read them, think of how the passages sound. Read them aloud. With what kind of voice do you read? What's your tone? Use your observation skills to choose the correct tone for each sentence or paragraph. Make sure you can support your answer with specific observations about point of view and word choice. Write your observations and notes on a separate sheet of paper. When you are finished, read the answers and explanations that follow.

1. I need to see you in my office the second this meeting is over!
   a. gloomy
   b. urgent
   c. bitter

2. If it's not too much trouble, do you think maybe you could come into my office after this meeting, if you don't mind?
   a. cheerful
   b. hopeful
   c. insecure

3. A person should not speak that way in front of his supervisor if he wishes to keep his job.
   a. threatening
   b. humorous
   c. sincere

4. You shouldn't say things like that in front of the boss. You could jeopardize your job.
   a. threatening
   b. humorous
   c. sincere

5. You have the biggest interview of your life scheduled for tomorrow morning at 9:00. You pick out your suit, iron a shirt, and polish your shoes. You double check the bus map and schedule. You set your alarm early so you can catch the 7:45 bus, which will get you there by 8:10, just in case. Then, during the night, a storm hits and knocks out the electricity. Your alarm doesn't go off, and you wake up . . . at 9:15.
   a. humorous
   b. ironic
   c. angry

6. I had the biggest interview of my life scheduled for Tuesday morning at 9:00. Monday night, I picked out my suit, ironed a shirt, and polished my shoes. I double checked the bus map and schedule. I set my alarm early so I could catch the 7:45 bus, which would get me there by 8:10, just in case. Then, during the night, a storm hit and knocked out the electricity. My alarm didn't go off and I woke up at 9:15. I can't believe it!

   a. sad

   b. disrespectful

   c. angry

Answers

1. b. Several things indicate an urgent tone: the word *need*, the phrase "the second this meeting is over," and the exclamation point all suggest immediacy and urgency.

2. c. This writer is insecure; "If it's not too much trouble, "do you think maybe," and "if you don't mind" show that this person is worried that the reader won't agree to what he desires.

3. a. The tone here is threatening. One clue is that the writer uses the third person to distance herself from the reader. If the writer were trying to be helpful, she would be more personal. This distance also suggests that the writer is "talking down to" the reader.

4. c. Here, the writer uses the second person to address the reader which immediately creates a feeling of closeness. There is nothing in this passage to indicate a threat or humor. The writer is simply being honest and sincere.

5. b. Irony is the mood created when things happen in a manner that is opposite of what was expected to happen. Here, the writer puts you in his shoes by using the second person pronoun "you" to describe a frustrating experience that readers can relate to. Because the writer uses "you," you get the feeling that he is describing an imaginary scenario rather than something he actually experienced, so you can't say the tone is angry. In addition, the ellipsis (. . .) holds off the final word to increase the sense of suspense and irony.

6. c. Here, the writer uses the first person point of view as if he is describing a real experience. If this is a real experience, he has a right to be upset and angry. The added sentence "I can't believe it" adds to the angry tone. In other words, the writer is saying, "I did so much to make sure I was there early. I didn't deserve this."

USING CONTEXT TO DETERMINE TONE

Let's take another look at the word that opened this chapter, *sure*. To determine the tone of this word, you need some context. See if you can determine the tone of *sure* in the context of this brief exchange:

> Seth: "Will you help me?"
> Amanda: "Sure. As soon as I'm done living."

Now, it should be clear that Amanda isn't about to stop what she's doing to help Seth. In fact, her second sentence suggests that she will *never* help Seth. The tone in which she says *sure* could best be described as sarcastic and disrespectful.

PRACTICE 2

Determine the tone for *sure* in the following passages:

1. Seth: "You'll help me, won't you?"
   Amanda: "Uh . . . sure, I guess . . . if you really want me to."
   a. indifferent
   b. reluctant
   c. playful
   d. sincere

2. Seth: "Are you going to help?"
   Amanda: "Sure thing! I'll be right there."
   a. urgent
   b. regretful
   c. uncertain
   d. enthusiastic

3. Seth: "I was going to tell you about it, but it just slipped my mind.
       I really meant to tell you."
   Amanda: "Yeah, right. Sure you did."
   a. skeptical
   b. critical
   c. threatening
   d. angry

Answers

1. The tone here is best described as **b**, reluctant. The "uh," ellipsis, "I guess," and "if you really want me to" all suggest that Amanda isn't terribly willing to help.
2. The tone here is best described as **d**, enthusiastic. The exclamation point and the fact that the speaker is going to be "right there" show Amanda's enthusiasm.
3. The tone here is best described as **a**, skeptical. The best clue is the first sentence, "Yeah, right," which shows that Amanda doesn't believe Seth.

HOW TONE CAN HELP YOU REMEMBER WHAT YOU READ

Determining tone is not just important for understanding what you read. It's also an important tool for remembering what you read. That's because tone, like visualization, adds another "sense" to your reading experience. Visualization helps you "see" what you read, so you're much more likely to remember it. Similarly, if you can see *and hear* what you read, you engage yet another sense in the reading experience.

As a result, you're more likely to remember what you read. If you can hear the writer's tone of voice, you can better remember what the writer is saying. And because tone is so closely related to the main idea, remembering the tone of voice can help you recall the main idea as well. Remember, both tone and the main idea show what the writer thinks or feels about her subject.

IN SHORT

Tone is the mood or attitude conveyed by words or speech. In writing, tone is suggested by word choice and point of view. Writers use tone to help convey meaning, so you need to look carefully for clues in the writer's language and style to determine how writers want their words to sound. An ability to determine tone will help you better understand and remember what you read.

Skill Building Until Next Time

1. Listen carefully to people today and notice how much you depend on tone to determine exactly what people mean when they speak to you. Notice also how you use tone to convey meaning when you speak to other people.
2. Go back to Practice 1, where you identified the tone of six passages. Change the tone of some of those passages.

CHAPTER | 18

Writers often spell out their main ideas in clear topic sentences. But what happens when they don't? This chapter will show you how to determine the main idea of a passage when the writer doesn't provide a topic sentence.

FINDING AN IMPLIED IDEA

When a crime is committed, detectives have to figure out who did it. They rely on a series of clues that lead them, directly or indirectly, to the answer. As a reader, you sometimes need to go through a similar process. When there's no topic sentence stating the main idea of the text, you need to look for clues to figure out the main idea.

LOOKING FOR CLUES

To find an implied main idea, you must make careful observations so that you can make a legitimate inference about the passage. It might take a little detective work, but now that you know how to find details and how word choice and point of view create tone, you can make observations that will enable you to find main ideas even when they're not explicitly stated. When there's no clear topic sentence stating the main idea, you can *create* one so that you can better remember what you read.

To review, a main idea:

- Says something about the subject
- Is general enough to serve as an "umbrella" for the rest of the sentences in the paragraph or passage
- Is an assertion that can be supported by details, examples, and explanations

PRACTICE 1

Take a look at the paragraph below. Read the paragraph carefully and answer the question that follows. On a separate sheet of paper, write down the observations that lead you to believe your answer is correct.

Four years ago when I joined this company, tuition reimbursement was 100 percent. Two years ago, it was cut down to 75 percent. Now they send us a memo that tuition reimbursement has been slashed to 50 percent.

There is no topic sentence in this paragraph. But you should be able to determine the writer's main idea from the facts she provides and from her tone. What do you think she is suggesting?

a. Tuition reimbursement is a waste of company money.
b. Soon there will be no tuition reimbursement at all.
c. 50 percent tuition reimbursement is excellent.

Answer

The best answer is **b**. Although the writer doesn't come right out and say it, she's suggesting that soon there won't be any tuition reimbursement at all. How can you tell this is the main idea? One clue is the writer's word choice. Look at the words she uses to describe the tuition reimbursement reductions:

Four years ago when I joined this company, tuition reimbursement was 100 percent. Two years ago, it was *cut down* to 75 percent. Now they send us a memo that tuition reimbursement has been *slashed* to 50 percent.

Certainly, if she believed that tuition reimbursement is a waste of company money (answer **a**), she wouldn't have used these words. Instead, she might have used the words *lowered*, *reduced*, or *minimized*—words with a neutral or positive connotation.

Another clue is the information in the paragraph. What do all of these ideas add up to? Collectively, what idea do they support? The only possible answer is **b**. Neither the first nor the last answer is suggested by all of the sentences in the paragraph.

Yet another clue is the phrase "Now they send us." The word "now" suggests a bit of disbelief or exasperation—a "not again!" In addition, the unnamed third person "they" sets up something of an "us vs. them" situation: the people who want the tuition reimbursement against those who want to reduce or eliminate it.

You also have to keep in mind the position of the writer. Who is writing this? Clearly the writer is an employee, someone who would benefit from full tuition reimbursement. Thus, it's not very likely that he or she would think tuition reimbursement is a waste. Further, **c** is not a good answer because the writer was around for 100 percent tuition reimbursement, so she's not likely to be happy with just half of that amount. In fact, the paragraph clearly conveys the idea that she is unhappy with the repeated cuts in tuition reimbursement.

PRACTICE 2

Now look at another paragraph about the same issue. Read it carefully and see if you can determine the implied main idea here:

Tuition reimbursement at our company has been reduced to 50 percent. At *Books & Company*, tuition reimbursement is just 40 percent. At *Metals Inc.* and *Glass Industries*, tuition reimbursement is only 50 percent and only for work related courses. And at *Burgers-to-Go* and *Do-nuts Galore* companies, there's no tuition reimbursement at all.

What is this writer suggesting?

    a. You should be glad you have 50 percent tuition reimbursement.
    b. You should go to another company.
    c. Soon there will be no tuition reimbursement at all.

Answer

The correct answer is **a**: The writer is suggesting that readers should be glad they have 50 percent tuition reimbursement. How can you tell? First of all, this is the only idea that all of the sentences support. It's the only choice that can serve as an umbrella for the paragraph. Each fact the writer offers shows that other companies offer even less tuition reimbursement. This shows that the reader is actually better off than employees at a lot of other companies. In addition, the words "just," "only" and "at all" emphasize that 50 percent is the highest tuition reimbursement amount around.

NOTE: If you had any trouble with these two passages, STOP. Review Chapters 6 and 7 and come back to this chapter later.

PRACTICE 3

Here's another passage to practice finding an implied main idea. This time, you won't be given choices. Instead, make observations about the passage and then on a separate sheet of paper write a topic sentence that expresses the main idea implied by the paragraph. Make sure it's a sentence that can serve as an umbrella for all of the ideas in the paragraph.

> Lloyd has been looking rather pale lately. I notice he's lost quite a bit of weight, too. When he talks to me lately, he avoids looking me in the eye. And when we got that memo about the new drug testing policy, he cursed quietly, tore it up, and threw it in the trash.

Answer

Your topic sentence should look something like this: *Lloyd may have a drug problem.* This is the idea that all of the sentences in the paragraph collectively suggest. A sentence like "There's something wrong with

Lloyd" might also seem like a good umbrella for this paragraph, but it's *too* general. It's a much wider umbrella than is needed. Your topic sentence should be general enough to cover the ideas in the paragraph but not so general that you could add dozens of other ideas. Thus, because everything the writer mentions in the paragraph could be a symptom of drug abuse, "Lloyd may have a drug problem" is a much better topic sentence for this paragraph.

In addition, notice that the tone of the paragraph is somewhat tentative. The writer doesn't come right out and say what he thinks. This could be because drug abuse is a serious problem. He doesn't want to outright accuse Lloyd, so he doesn't offer a topic sentence.

Practice 4

Now look at a paragraph where word choice, point of view, and tone play a bigger role in determining the main idea. Read the paragraph carefully and list your observations on a separate sheet of paper. What do you notice about the language in this paragraph? What details and descriptions does the writer provide? After you write down several observations, answer the question below.

> My "office" measures a whopping 5 feet by 7 feet. A large desk is squeezed into one corner, leaving just enough room for a rickety chair between the desk and the wall. Yellow paint is peeling off the walls in dirty chunks. The ceiling is barely six feet tall; it's like a hat that I wear all day long. The window, a single 2 x 2 pane, looks out onto a solid brick wall just two feet away.

What is the main idea implied by this paragraph?

   a. This office is small but comfortable.
   b. This office is in need of repair.
   c. This office is old and claustrophobic.

Answer

Only sentence **c** expresses an appropriate main idea for this paragraph. The details of the office show that it's so small, it's suffocating. First of all, the writer puts "office" in quotation marks. This suggests that it's not even suitable to be called an office. Second, the writer uses the word "whopping" to describe the room's dimensions. Did you "hear" the sarcastic tone that "whopping" creates?

In addition, you are given the specific detail that the room is only 5 x 7 feet and the vivid comparison between the ceiling and a hat. True, the office is in need of some repair (the paint is peeling off the walls), but that idea isn't general enough to serve as an umbrella for this paragraph. The need for repairs and the word "rickety" do suggest the office is old.

HOW FINDING AN IMPLIED MAIN IDEA HELPS YOU REMEMBER

Of course, the ability to find an implied main idea is as important to reading retention as being able to find a clearly stated main idea. Remember, ideas in paragraphs work to support a larger idea that holds them together, and paragraphs work together to support an overall main idea in the larger text. Finding the main idea enables you to remember the most important parts of what you read.

IN SHORT

Many writers use implication or suggestion to convey their ideas rather than directly stating them. Finding the implied main idea requires a little detective work, but it is not as difficult as you may have thought, now that you know more about language and the way words can be used to suggest ideas. When there's no clear topic sentence, look for an idea that can serve as an umbrella for all of the ideas in the passage. Look at the word choices and point of view and listen for the tone of the passage.

Skill Building Until Next Time

1. Listen carefully to people today. Are there times when they *imply* things without directly saying them? Are there times when *you* use suggestion to get your ideas across? How do you do this? Be aware of how you and others use indirect language and suggestion to convey meaning.

2. Write a paragraph that does not have a topic sentence. You should have a clear idea of the main idea before you write your paragraph and make sure your sentences use language that will help your readers understand your main idea. For example, think of a topic sentence about the kind of person you are, but don't write it down. Then, write several sentences that support your topic sentence with language that leads your reader to the proper conclusion. You may want to show your paragraph to others to see if they can correctly guess your main idea.

CHAPTER | 19

The capstone strategy for understanding and remembering what you read is to take a writer's ideas and put them into your own words. This chapter will show you how to summarize and paraphrase what you read.

PUTTING IT IN YOUR OWN WORDS

A sure sign that you understand something is that you can explain it to someone else. Similarly, if you really understand something you read, you should be able to "rewrite" it. And rewriting what you read is a sure way to help you remember it.

This doesn't mean, of course, that you should sit down and copy a book cover to cover. That wouldn't serve any purpose. It does mean, however, that you take the ideas in the text you're reading and put those ideas *into your own words*. You can do this by *summarizing* or *paraphrasing* what you read.

WRITING A SUMMARY

Back in Chapter 8, you learned how to gloss by taking the main idea, reducing it, and rewriting it in the margin. When you glossed, you simply found the central idea in the topic sentence and more or less copied it. The point of this chapter is to summarize the main idea *in your own words* as much as possible.

Why? Because writing the main idea in your own words requires you to *process* the information instead of just copying it. In other words, you need to take the ideas and information and make sense of it in your own way. By digesting the information like this, you give it a strong, solid hold in your memory.

Guidelines for Summarizing

Summarizing will benefit you most if you keep in mind the following guidelines:

- Work only with the main ideas and most important supporting points.
- There's no definite rule, but in general, summaries should be about one fourth the length of the original text. Thus, if you have a four-sentence paragraph, for example, your summary should be about one sentence long. Four or five paragraphs should be summarized in about one paragraph. A 40 page chapter, however, could probably be summarized effectively in four pages.
- Keep main ideas in the same order.
- Be careful not to change any of the writer's facts or ideas.

If this seems like a big challenge, just imagine how you would explain the key ideas in a passage to a friend. Then, write that explanation down in your own words, in your own way. Of course, you don't need to change key terms, but the rest of your summary should be as much in your own words as possible.

PRACTICE 1

Take another look at the passage you saw earlier about Sigmund Freud's personality theory. Beneath the first paragraph is a sample summary of that paragraph. After you read the sample paragraph, summarize the other paragraphs. For now, don't worry if you don't change *every* word. Obviously, key terms will stay the same. But do put the ideas in your own words as much as possible.

> Sigmund Freud, the famous psychiatrist, made many contributions to the science of psychology. One of his greatest contributions was his theory of the personality. According to Freud, the human personality is made up of three parts: the id, the ego, and the superego.

Sample Summary:
> Freud's theory of the three parts of the human personality has been very important in psychology.

, Here are the rest of the paragraphs for you to summarize. Write a one-sentence summary in your own words for each paragraph on a separate sheet of paper.

> The id is the part of the personality that exists only in the subconscious. According to Freud, the id has no direct contact with reality. It is the innermost core of our personality and operates according to the pleasure principle. That is, it seeks immediate gratification for its desires, regardless of external realities or consequences. It is not even aware that external realities or consequences exist.
> The ego develops from the id and is the part of the personality in contact with the real world. The ego is conscious and therefore aims to satisfy the subconscious desires of the id as best it can within the individual's environment. When it can't satisfy those desires, it tries to control or suppress the id. The ego functions according to the reality principle.
> The superego is the third and final part of the personality to develop. This is the part of the personality that contains our moral values and ideals, our notion of what's right and wrong. The superego gives us the "rules" that help the ego control the id. For example, a child wants a toy that belongs

to another child (id). He checks his environment to see if it's possible to take that toy (ego). He can, and does. But then he remembers that it's wrong to take something that belongs to someone else (superego), and returns the toy to the other child.

Answer

Answers will vary. Here's one summary of these paragraphs. Notice how the sentences have been put together to form one paragraph summarizing the whole passage:

> Freud's theory of the three parts of the human personality has been very important in psychology. The subconscious id is driven by the pleasure principle. The ego, which operates in the real world (reality principle), tries to satisfy the id. The superego provides the ego with morals and values to do what's right.

Use Glossing and Highlighting to Help You Summarize

Rather than summarizing each paragraph as soon as you read it, try doing it this way: First, underline, highlight, or gloss each paragraph. Then use your underlining, highlighting, or glossing to write a paragraph summarizing the whole passage.

Take a look at this example. The passage about different types of burns has been highlighted below. Notice how the sample summary that follows it pulls from information that is highlighted in the passage.

> **There are three different kinds of burns:** first degree, second degree, and third degree. **Each type of burn requires a different type of medical treatment.**
>
> The least serious burn is the **first degree burn.** This burn **causes the skin to turn red but does not cause blistering.** A mild sunburn is a good example of a first-degree burn, and, like a mild sunburn, first-degree burns **generally do not require medical treatment** other than a gentle cooling of the burned skin with ice or cold tap water.

Second degree burns, on the other hand, **do cause blistering of the skin and should be treated immediately.** These burns should **be immersed in warm water and then wrapped in a sterile dressing or bandage.** (Do not apply butter or grease to these burns; despite the old wives' tale, butter does not help burns heal and actually increases the chances of infection.) If second degree burns cover a large part of the body, then the victim should be taken to the hospital immediately for medical care.

Third degree burns are those that **char the skin and turn it black or burn so deeply that the skin shows white.** These burns usually result from direct contact with flames and have a great chance of becoming infected. **All third degree burn victims should receive immediate hospital care.** Burns should not be immersed in water, and charred clothing should not be removed from the victim as it may also remove skin. If possible a sterile dressing or bandage should be applied to burns before the victim is transported to the hospital.

Sample Summary:

Each of the three types of burns should be treated differently. Because first degree burns do not blister, they do not need medical attention. A burn that blisters is a second degree burn and must be soaked in warm water, then dressed with a sterile bandage. If the skin is charred (third degree burn), the victim should go to the hospital immediately.

PRACTICE 2

The passage below may be a little more difficult, since the ideas are not presented in neat paragraphs with clear topic sentences. Re-read this news article about the toxic chemical leak and decide what the main ideas and key pieces of information are. Highlight, underline, or gloss the passage. Then, summarize the article in a paragraph on a separate sheet of paper. Remember, minor supporting facts and specific details don't belong in a summary. Stick to the main ideas and most important facts.

ABC Chemical of Williamsburg, Ohio, is in hot water. Local environmentalists discovered last week that the company's plant has been leaking toxic chemicals into the town's water supply.

Records indicate that there has been a large increase in stomach ailments and short-term memory loss in the area.

The company spokesperson, Mel Gerardi, insists that ABC Chemical executives knew nothing of the leak. According to Gerardi, the company passed the city's Environmental Commission inspection just last month. How the leak went undetected, he says, is a mystery.

Local residents have threatened ABC Chemical with a class-action suit for negligence.

A similar case is pending in Richdale, Arkansas, where a pesticide company was found to have been emitting toxic fumes into the neighborhood. For several weeks, residents had complained of stomach pain and general nausea as well as difficulty remembering things. The cause was eventually traced back to the pesticide plant.

Answer

Answers will vary. Here's one sample summary:

Residents in an Ohio town have been sickened by toxic chemicals leaked by a local chemical company into the town's water supply. The leak was not detected in a recent inspection. Residents are suing the company for negligence. A pesticide company in Arkansas is also being sued for sickening residents with toxic fumes.

PARAPHRASING

Although summarizing is the strategy to choose when you want to focus on the main idea, when a passage is particularly difficult, you'll often benefit more from *paraphrasing*. To paraphrase means to take someone else's ideas and restate them in your own words. The main difference between paraphrasing and summarizing is that a paraphrase isn't limited to the main idea. When you paraphrase a paragraph, you put *each idea* in that paragraph into your own words, whether it's the main idea, a major supporting idea, or minor support. Thus, you can be sure you understand an idea before you try to remember it.

Whereas a summary is usually no more than one fourth the size of its source, a paraphrase should be the *same size* as the original. That is, if you're paraphrasing a paragraph with five sentences, your paraphrase should also contain about five sentences. That's because you are not cutting out minor supporting ideas and details.

The important thing to watch out for when paraphrasing is not to change the writer's ideas. Often when readers process information like this, it's easy to include their own feelings about the topic in their paraphrase. But when you summarize or paraphrase, you need to stick to what the writer is saying. Save *your own* ideas for your notes and comments in the margin.

Paraphrase Ideas, Not Words

The key to a good paraphrase is to work idea by idea, not word by word. The trouble with going word by word is that you're likely to simply substitute one word for another (synonyms) without really making the ideas your own. Read a sentence, understand the whole idea it conveys, and *then* put that idea into your own words just like you did for your summaries. See the following example to get you started.

Original sentence:

Under managed care systems, more and more emphasis is being placed on pre-care and post-care, which means placing more and more responsibility for healthcare delivery in the hands of allied health workers.

Poor paraphrase (synonym substitution):

In managed care programs, greater and greater stress is put on care before and after illnesses. As a result, greater and greater responsibility for these services is given to workers in allied health.

Good paraphrase:

> Increasingly, allied health workers are doing more as HMOs
> focus on preventative care and follow-up treatments.

Notice that the good paraphrase is much more "processed" than the poor one. It has a different structure as well as different words.

You'll keep away from synonym substitution if you don't look right at the text as you're trying to paraphrase it. That is, once you understand the idea, put the text aside. *Then* paraphrase. If you have it right in front of you, you may be tempted to substitute synonyms.

PRACTICE 3

Scientific texts are often difficult to follow. Try paraphrasing the following sentences to make sure you clearly understand them:

1. Evolution changes the genetic make-up of populations gradually over time, and greater complexity and adaptability do occur.

2. The human species is unique in its great ability to control factors that limit population growth in other species, and our species has therefore been growing exponentially for hundreds of years.

Answers

Answers will vary. Here are sample paraphrases:
1. Species can become more adaptable and complex through evolution, which is the slow change of a group's genetic structure.
2. Unlike other species, humans have conquered many of the problems that keep population growth rates low. As a result, the number of human beings on this planet has been increasing at a phenomenal rate for several centuries.

IN SHORT

To summarize and paraphrase, you need to understand the ideas and information in the text and put those ideas into your own words. Summaries should include only the main ideas and most important supporting ideas. A paraphrase, on the other hand, should include all of the writer's ideas. Use summaries to remember the most important information in what you read. Paraphrase to help you understand difficult sentences or ideas.

Skill Building Until Next Time

1. Write a brief summary of this chapter on a separate sheet of paper.
2. If you come across any difficult sentences in your reading this week, paraphrase them. Take each idea and put it into your own words.

CHAPTER | 20

This last chapter reviews the strategies you learned in Chapters 15–20: analyzing word choice and point of view, determining tone, finding the implied main idea, summarizing, and paraphrasing. You'll put all of this knowledge to practice in a review that brings in all the strategies you've learned throughout this book.

PUTTING IT ALL TOGETHER

Congratulations! You're in the home stretch. You've been building your reading skills chapter by chapter throughout this book, and now it's time to pull your skills all together in a final review. Here is one long passage in which you'll practice strategies from this section as well as sections 1–3. But first, here's a review of what you've learned in this section.

IN BRIEF

- **Chapter 16: Word Choice and Point of View.** Writers choose their words carefully to reflect their attitude towards their subject. You learned how to look for clues in word choice and point of view to make inferences about the writer's attitude.

- **Chapter 17: Determining Tone.** You learned how word choice and point of view work together to create tone. Tone is the mood or attitude conveyed by words or speech. You practiced recognizing a variety of different tones of voice and made observations to support your inferences and boost your retention.
- **Chapter 18: Finding an Implied Main Idea.** You learned how to work like a detective and find clues to determine the main idea when the writer doesn't provide clear topic sentences. You looked at word choice, point of view, and tone to see what main idea all of the other sentences in the passage added up to.
- **Chapter 19: Putting It in Your Own Words.** You practiced two powerful reading strategies: summarizing and paraphrasing. You learned how to "process" what you read and "translate" those ideas into your own words. When you summarized, you focused on the main idea and key support and put them into your own words. When you paraphrased, you rewrote sentences idea by idea.

If any of these terms or strategies sound unfamiliar to you, STOP. Take a few minutes to review the chapter or concept that is unclear.

Practice

Here's one long passage about taxes. Pre-read first, and then answer the pre-reading question. Then, read the passage carefully. Keep in mind the following points, which are essential parts of this exercise:

- You may use your vocabulary list, but not a dictionary.
- As you read, write your questions and reactions in the margin.
- Highlight or underline the text as you read.

Pre-Reading Question:

1. Based on your pre-reading, what do you expect to learn from this passage? On a separate sheet of paper, write several questions that you expect the passage to answer.

Change the Tax System

Every year, April 15th comes around like a recurring nightmare. Citizens brace themselves for the agony of complicated forms and hours of gathering numbers and receipts to figure out how much more of their hard-earned money they'll be forced to give to Uncle Sam. It's a task and a system that citizens loathe, and it's time for a serious restructuring of the U.S. tax system.

Citizens are currently being taxed for working hard and saving money—two activities we should encourage. Instead, citizens should be taxed for the "bad" things that they do. That is, they should be taxed on the things that deplete our natural resources, pollute our environment, and create waste. These taxes fall into three categories: taxes on energy consumption, taxes on health deterrents, and taxes on luxury. At the same time that these taxes are increased, taxes on earnings and savings should be reduced proportionately.

Taxes on Energy Consumption

The gasoline that we put in our cars pollutes the air and drains our natural resources. Traffic jams clog our streets and create noise pollution. A higher tax on gasoline, on oil, and on cars and car parts would encourage people to conserve gas, to carpool, to use public transportation, and to walk or ride bicycles when possible. Citizens would then benefit from cleaner air and healthier bodies.

Electricity and other forms of energy should also be taxed at higher rates to help us conserve our natural resources. Increased taxes on electricity would encourage people to turn off lights and appliances when not in use. In addition, it would discourage people from buying gadgets they don't need, like salad shooters and electronic calendars. Citizens would hang their clothes to dry more often instead of running the dryer, would use a regular toothbrush instead of an electric one, and would cook their food in ovens rather than the microwave (a much healthier choice).

Taxes on Health Deterrents

Cigarettes and alcohol are already taxed—but they should be taxed more. The tremendous burden in health care costs created by these habits alone should warrant higher taxes on these addictive substances. Higher taxes on cigarettes and alcohol will help reduce the number of people addicted to these substances. Children and teens will be less able to afford these items, and adults will consider whether their habit is really worth the hole it's burning in their pocket. We'll have a healthier population and reduce overall health care costs.

Taxes on Luxury

Despite America's large middle class, a great majority of wealth in this country is still in the hands of a very few. Those citizens who are wealthy enough to afford such luxury purchases as jet airplanes, yachts, summer and winter homes, car collections, fur coats, jewels, and other unnecessary items should pay higher taxes on these purchases. That way, citizens who have to struggle just to put food on the table can be taxed less.

Benefits for Everybody

Even if the average citizen ends up paying the same amount in taxes, the system should still be changed to tax the bad, not the good. Taxpayers would certainly feel much better about giving money to Uncle Sam, and who knows? We might get a few people to break a few bad habits in the process.

2. What does *recurring* (paragraph 1) mean?
   a. happening over and over
   b. current
   c. very bad, frightening
3. What does *warrant* (paragraph 5) mean?
   a. explain
   b. arrest
   c. justify

4. What is the overall main idea of this passage? State it in your own words.

5. How is this passage organized?
   a. cause and effect
   b. most important to least important
   c. analysis/classification
6. Identify two opinions.
7. What is the tone of paragraph 1?
   a. apologetic
   b. indignant
   c. demanding
8. Summarize this passage in one paragraph.

Answers

1. From the headings in the passage, you might expect to get answers to the following questions:
   • Why change the tax system?
   • How should the tax system be changed?
   • What kind of taxes are there on energy consumption? (What falls into this category of "energy consumption"?)
   • What kind of taxes are there on health deterrents? (What are these "health deterrents"?)
   • What kind of taxes should there be on health deterrents?
   • What kind of taxes are there on luxury? (What is considered "luxury"?)
   • What kind of taxes should there be on luxury?
   • What benefits will there be for everybody?
2. a. *Recurring* means *happening over and over*. Tax time comes around every year, without fail.
3. c. *Warrant* means *justify*. The paragraph says that smoking and drinking create a large burden on health care costs, and the writer suggests that this is reason enough to raise taxes on these items.
4. The overall main idea of this passage, stated in the second paragraph, might be restated as follows: The tax system should be restructured so people are taxed for wasting, not for working.
5. The passage is organized by analysis/classification, **c.** The writer

explains the different groups of taxes. The sentence "These taxes fall into three categories" should help you anticipate this organizational pattern.

6. Opinions include the following sentences: "It's a task and a system that citizens loathe, and it's time for a serious restructuring of the U.S. tax system"; "two activities we should encourage"; and "citizens should be taxed for the 'bad' things that they do." In fact, most of this passage is opinion. You should *not* have underlined sentences like "The gasoline that we put in our cars pollutes the air and drains our natural resources."

7. The tone of paragraph 1 is **b**, indignant. Words like "recurring nightmare," "brace themselves," "agony," and especially "how much more of their hard-earned money they'll be *forced* to give to Uncle Sam" clearly suggest that the writer feels indignant (angry about something thought to be unjust or unfair).

8. Answers will vary. Here's one summary of the passage:

> The U.S. tax system, which currently punishes citizens by taxing them for money they earn and save, should tax citizens for what they consume instead. Taxes on gas, electricity and other forms of energy should be raised to encourage citizens to conserve these resources. Taxes on cigarettes and alcohol should also be raised to discourage smoking and drinking and reduce health care costs. Taxes on luxury items should also be raised to reduce wasteful spending. Meanwhile, taxes on earnings and savings should be reduced, so citizens can feel better about how they're being taxed.

In addition, here's an example of how you might have underlined and reacted to the first part of the passage:

Change the Tax System

I dread 4/15! —— Every year, April 15th comes around like a recurring nightmare. Citizens brace themselves for the agony of complicated forms and hours of gathering numbers and receipts to figure out how much more of their hard-earned money they'll be forced to

yes, bu
the sho
form is
pretty
easy

give to Uncle Sam. <u>It's a task and a system that citizens loathe, and it's time for a serious restructuring of the U.S. tax system.</u>

    <u>Citizens are currently being taxed for working hard and saving money</u>—two activities we should encourage. <u>Instead,</u> *I agree* <u>citizens should be taxed for the "bad" things that they do.</u> */ I hadn't thought of it like this before* That is, they should be taxed on the things that deplete our natural resources, pollute our environment, and create waste. These taxes fall into three categories: taxes on energy consumption, taxes on health deterrents, and taxes on luxury. <u>At the same time that these taxes are increased, taxes on</u> — *That would be nice* <u>earnings and savings should be reduced proportionately.</u>

Taxes on Energy Consumption
The gasoline that we put in our cars pollutes the air and drains our natural resources. Traffic jams clog our streets and create noise pollution. A higher tax on gasoline, on oil, and on cars and car parts <u>would encourage people to conserve gas,</u> to carpool, to use public transportation, and to walk or ride bicycles when possible. <u>Citizens would then benefit from cleaner air and healthier bodies.</u>

True, but then I couldn't drive to work by myself every day

If you missed	Then review
Question 1	Chapter 1
Question 2	Chapter 4
Question 3	Chapter 4
Question 4	Chapter 6
Question 5	Chapter 11
Question 6	Chapter 12
Question 7	Chapter 17
Question 8	Chapter 19

Congratulations!

You've completed 20 chapters and are now better able to understand and remember what you read. Good work. Go ahead and take the post-test to see how much your reading skills have improved

Suggestions for how to continue improving your reading skills, along with a list of suggested books organized by subject appears in Appendix A.

Appendix B offers four charts: common prefixes, suffixes, Latin word roots, and Greek word roots. Studying these charts will help you to increase your vocabulary, which in turn will help you to understand more of what you read.

Now it's time to reward yourself for a job well done. Buy yourself a good book and enjoy!

POST-TEST

If you'd like to gauge how much your reading comprehension and retention skills have improved since you started this book, try this post-test. Though the questions are different from the pretest, the format is the same, so you will be able to directly compare results. The only key difference between these two tests is that the post-test uses more of the vocabulary words you've learned throughout this book.

When you complete this test, grade yourself, and then compare your pre- and post-test scores. If you scored much higher on the post-test, congratulations; you've profited noticeably from your hard work. If your score shows little improvement, perhaps there are certain chapters you need to review. Do you notice a pattern to the types of questions you got wrong?

Whatever your score on this post-test, keep this book around for review. Refer to it whenever you need tips on how to better understand and remember what you read.

Circle the correct answers below, or if this book doesn't belong to you, write the numbers 1–30 on a piece of paper and record your answers there.

Take as much time as you need to complete this post-test (plan on about a half an hour). When you finish, check your answers against the answer key that follows this test. Each answer tells you which chapters correspond to the strategies in that question.

Good luck!

Note: Do not use a dictionary for this post-test.

PART I

1. Before you read, you should:
    a. Set a time limit for your reading.
    b. Break up your reading into manageable tasks.
    c. Read the introduction and skim the section headings.
    d. (a) and (c)
    e. (b) and (c)
2. A dictionary definition typically includes:
    a. the main meaning of the word and variations of that word
    b. the part of speech and various meanings of the word
    c. the meaning of the word and related words
    d. the context in which the word is used
3. The *main idea* of a text is:
    a. an assertion that requires support
    b. support for the topic sentence
    c. a transition
    d. all of the above
4. The *subject* of a text is the same as the *main idea*.
    a. true
    b. false
    c. sometimes true

5. To *gloss* a text, you should:
   a. highlight key terms
   b. rewrite the major supporting ideas in each paragraph
   c. briefly summarize the main idea of each paragraph
   d. paraphrase each paragraph
6. To *highlight* a text, you should:
   a. highlight key terms
   b. highlight unfamiliar words
   c. highlight main ideas and major supporting ideas
   d. (a) and (c)
   e. (a) and (b)
7. A *topic sentence* is often:
   a. the point of view
   b. a supporting idea
   c. the first or last sentence in a paragraph
   d. a transitional sentence
8. Which of the following generally determines the *tone* of a passage?
   a. the topic sentence
   b. the author's opinions
   c. the word choice and point of view
   d. the organizational strategy
9. A *paraphrase* should be:
   a. about the same length as the text being paraphrased
   b. about ¼ the size of the text being paraphrased
   c. about twice as long as the text being paraphrased
   d. the text copied word for word
10. The *first person point of view*:
    a. creates distance and appears objective
    b. puts the reader in the writer's shoes
    c. addresses the reader directly
    d. is personal and subjective

PART II
Read the passages below carefully and answer the questions that follow.

Passage 1

The sentences are numbered to make the questions easier to follow.

(1) There are many things you can do to make tax time easier. (2) The single most important strategy is to keep accurate records. (3) Keep all of your pay stubs, receipts, bank statements, and other relevant financial information in a neat, organized folder so that when you're ready to prepare your form, all of your paperwork is in one place. (4) The second thing you can do is start early. (5) Get your tax forms from the post office as soon as they are available and start calculating. (6) This way, if you run into any problems, you have plenty of time to straighten them out. (7) You can also save time by reading the directions carefully. (8) This will prevent time-consuming errors. (9) Finally, if your taxes are relatively simple (you don't have itemized deductions or special investments), use the shorter tax form. (10) It's only one page, and if your records are in order, it can be completed in less than an hour.

11. The main idea of this passage is expressed in which sentence?
  a. 1
  b. 3
  c. 7
  d. 10

12. This paragraph uses which of the following organizational strategies?
  a. cause and effect
  b. analysis/classification
  c. order of importance
  d. chronology

13. This passage uses which point of view?
  a. first person
  b. second person
  c. third person
  d. first and second person

14. How many suggestions for tax time does this passage offer?

   a. one

   b. two

   c. three

   d. four

15. The sentence "It's only one page, and if your records are in order, it can be completed in less than an hour" is:

   a. the main idea of the passage

   b. a major supporting idea

   c. a minor supporting idea

   d. a transitional sentence

16. A good summary of this passage would be:

   a. Simple strategies can make tax time less taxing.

   b. Don't procrastinate at tax time.

   c. Always keep good records.

   d. Get a tax attorney.

17. According to the passage, who should use the shorter tax form?

   a. Everybody.

   b. People who do not have complicated finances.

   c. People who do have complicated finances.

   d. People who wait until the last minute to file taxes.

18. The sentence "The single most important strategy is to keep accurate records" is a:

   a. fact

   b. opinion

   c. both

   d. neither

19. Which is the most effective <u>underlining</u> of the following passage?

   a. You can also <u>save time</u> by reading the directions carefully. This will prevent time-consuming <u>errors</u>. Finally, <u>if your taxes are relatively simple</u> (you don't have itemized deductions or special investments), <u>use the shorter tax form</u>. It's only one page, and <u>if your records are in order</u>, it can be completed in <u>less</u> than an hour.

   b. You can also save time by <u>reading the directions carefully</u>. This will prevent time-consuming errors. Finally, if your taxes are relatively simple (<u>you don't have itemized deductions or special</u>

investments), use the shorter tax form. <u>It's only one page</u>, and if your records are in order, it can be completed in less than an hour.

c. You can also save time by <u>reading the directions carefully</u>. This will prevent time-consuming errors. Finally, if your taxes are relatively simple (you don't have itemized deductions or special investments), <u>use the shorter tax form</u>. It's only one page, and if your records are in order, it can be completed in less than an hour.

d. You can also <u>save time</u> by reading the directions carefully. This will prevent time-consuming errors. Finally, if your taxes are <u>relatively simple</u> (you don't have itemized deductions or special investments), use the shorter tax form. It's only one page, and if your records are in order, it can be completed in <u>less than an hour</u>.

PASSAGE 2

The following passage is excerpted from Jane Jacobs's 1961 book, *The Death and Life of Great American Cities*. The paragraphs are numbered to make the questions easier to follow.

(1) A city sidewalk by itself is nothing. It is an abstraction. It means something only in conjunction with the buildings and other uses that border it, or border other sidewalks very near it. The same might be said of streets, in the sense that they serve other purposes besides carrying wheeled traffic in their middles. Streets and their sidewalks, the main public places of a city, are its most vital organs. Think of a city and what comes to mind? Its streets. If a city's streets look interesting, the city looks interesting; if they look dull, the city looks dull.

(2) More than that, and here we get down to the first problem, if a city's streets are safe from barbarism and fear, the city is thereby tolerably safe from barbarism and fear. When people say that a city, or a part of it, is dangerous or is a jungle, what they mean primarily is that they do not feel safe on the sidewalks.

(3) But sidewalks and those who use them are not passive beneficiaries of safety or helpless victims of danger. Sidewalks, their bordering uses, and their users, are active participants in the drama of civilization versus barbarism in cities. To keep the city safe is a fundamental task of a city's streets and its sidewalks.

(4) This task is totally unlike any service that sidewalks and streets in little towns or true suburbs are called upon to do. Great cities are not like towns, only larger. They are not like suburbs, only denser. They differ from towns and suburbs in basic ways, and one of these is that cities are, by definition, full of strangers. . . .

(5) The bedrock attribute of a successful city district is that a person must feel personally safe and secure on the street among all these strangers. He must not feel automatically menaced by them. A city district that fails in this respect also does badly in other ways and lays up for itself, and for its city at large, mountain on mountain of trouble.

20. According to the passage, cities are different from towns because:
   a. they are much bigger
   b. they have crowded streets
   c. most people are unfriendly
   d. most people are strangers

21. According to the passage, a city district is successful if:
   a. its streets are clean
   b. people feel safe on the streets
   c. people feel safe in their houses
   d it feels like the suburbs

22. The word "menaced" (paragraph 5) means:
   a. threatened
   b. disliked
   c. rejected
   d. nervous

23. According to the passage, the state of a city sidewalk shows:
   a. the neglect of the people who live on that block
   b. the politicians who govern that district of the city
   c. the health of that part of the city
   d. the battle between safety and danger
   e. (a) and (d)

24. A good paraphrase of the last sentence in paragraph 1 is:
   a. Cities can look both interesting and dull.
   b. Look carefully at city streets and sidewalks.
   c. A city is reflected in its streets.
   d. Avoid dull city streets.

25. A good glossing of paragraph 2 would be:
    a. streets need to be safe for city to be safe.
    b. city is a jungle.
    c. people don't feel safe on streets.
    d. city streets are the problem.
26. Based on the passage, what would you expect the next few paragraphs to do?
    a. provide examples of safe city streets
    b. offer ideas for how to keep sidewalks clean
    c. offer ideas for how to work with local politicians to keep streets safe
    d. provide examples of the kinds of problems cities face when streets are unsafe
27. According to the passage, the city:
    a. is a jungle
    b. is defined by its streets
    c. is menacing
    d. is more dense than suburbs
28. The word "barbarism" in paragraph 2 means:
    a. criminals
    b. rudeness
    c. brutality
    d. danger
29. The tone of this passage suggests that:
    a. People underestimate the role of city streets.
    b. People spend too much time on sidewalks and streets.
    c. People need to take better care of sidewalks.
    d. Sidewalks are a serious problem in cities.
30. The main idea of paragraph 3 is which sentence?
    a. But sidewalks and those who use them are not passive beneficiaries of safety or helpless victims of danger.
    b. Sidewalks, their bordering uses, and their users, are active participants in the drama of civilization versus barbarism in cities.
    c. To keep the city safe is a fundamental task of a city's streets and its sidewalks.

ANSWER KEY

Question	Answer	Chapter
1.	e	1
2.	b	3
3.	a	6
4.	b	6
5.	c	8
6.	d	8
7.	c	6
8.	c	16, 17
9.	a	19
10.	d	16
11.	a	6
12.	c	11
13.	b	16
14.	d	2
15.	c	7
16.	a	8, 19
17.	b	2
18.	b	12
19.	c	8
20.	d	2
21.	b	2
22.	a	4
23.	c	2
24.	c	19
25.	a	8
26.	d	11, 19
27.	b	2
28.	c	4
29.	a	18
30.	c	6

APPENDIX A:
ADDITIONAL RESOURCES

Reading is like exercise: If you don't keep doing it, you'll get out of shape. Like muscles that grow stronger with each repetition, your reading skills will grow stronger and stronger with each text that you read actively. But if you stop working out, your reading muscles will deteriorate, and you may find yourself struggling with material that you could have easily understood several months ago.

So don't stop now! You've really just begun. Understanding and remembering what you read are skills to build throughout your lifetime.

TIPS FOR CONTINUING TO IMPROVE YOUR READING SKILLS

Here are several ways you can continue to strengthen your reading skills:

- **Read!** Read anything and everything—books, newspapers, magazines, novels, and poems. The more you read, the better. Set yourself a reading goal: one book a month, two books while you're on vacation, a half hour of reading every night before bed. There's a list of suggested books at the end of this section; try some.
- **Tell others about what you read.** Summarize the main ideas of whatever you read for someone who might be interested.
- **Take notes on what you read.** You should always take notes, but they are especially important when you check books out from the library. You never know when that information will come in handy after you've returned the books.
- **Continue to add to your vocabulary list.** Review your vocabulary list on a regular basis and keep adding new words all the time. Teach others new words that you learn.
- **Discover new authors.** Check out the best-seller list in your newspaper or at your local bookstore and read one of the books on that list. If it's a best seller, it's probably a book that appeals to a wide variety of readers, and chances are good that you'll like it.
- **Spend time in book stores and libraries.** There are bound to be books and authors that appeal to some of your interests. Don't be afraid to ask a salesperson or librarian to help you. Describe your interests and your preferences so they can help you find books you'll enjoy reading.
- **Take a course at a local college.** Most courses (other than mathematics and computer science) require a significant amount of reading, so they're a great way to sharpen your reading skills while you work towards a degree or a greater understanding of a certain subject. In addition, if you're in a class, you'll have a teacher who can guide you to make sure you correctly comprehend and remember the ideas in what you read.
- **Make reading a family project.** For example, if your children have a reading contest or a book drive, read a book for each book they read. Go with them to the library and choose a book for yourself

each time you go. The more your children see you reading, the more likely they are to become interested in reading as well, and strong reading skills are a key to success in school. In addition, ask your children questions about what they read. Help them remember more by talking about their reading.

- **Join a reading group.** Most cities and towns have clubs that meet every two weeks or each month to discuss a selected book. In these groups, you'll get to discuss your ideas and questions with a group of friends and associates in an informal setting. If your area doesn't have a reading group, start your own. You and your friends can take turns choosing which books you'll read and discuss.

- **Review this book and your notes from this book periodically to refresh your memory**. Remember, repetition is the key to mastery.

SUGGESTED READING LIST

Below is a list of books organized by subject. Choose a category that interests you and try some of the books listed there.

Science Fiction

Fahrenheit 451 by Ray Bradbury

The Island of Dr. Moreau by H. G. Wells

The Left Hand of Darkness by Ursula LeGuin

Stranger in a Strange Land by Robert Heinlein

1984 by George Orwell

Jurassic Park, The Lost World, Timeline and other novels by Michael Crighton

Do Androids Dream of Electric Sheep? by Philip K. Dick

The Time Machine by H. G. Wells

Brave New World by Aldous Huxley

The Harry Potter series by J. K. Rowling

Science/Medicine

The Lives of a Cell by Lewis Thomas

Mortal Lessons by Richard Selzer

Virus Hunter by C. J. Peters and Mark Olshaker

Horror/Fantasy

Dr. Jekyll and Mr. Hyde by Robert Louis Stevenson

The Stand and other novels by Stephen King

Stories by Edgar Allen Poe

The Hobbit by J.R.R. Tolkien

On a Pale Horse by Piers Anthony

Autobiography/Memoir

Angela's Ashes and *'Tis* by Frank McCourt

The Autobiography of Malcolm X by Malcolm X

The Story of My Life by Helen Keller

The Diary of Anne Frank by Anne Frank

Night by Elie Weisel

The Heroic Slave by Frederick Douglas

I Know Why the Caged Bird Sings by Maya Angelou

Having Our Say by Sarah L. and Elizabeth Delaney

Black Boy by Richard Wright

Everything I Need to Know I Learned in Kindergarten by Robert Fulghum

Tuesdays with Morrie by Mitch Albam

Historical/Social Issues

Of Mice and Men by John Steinbeck

The Color Purple by Alice Walker

The Last of the Mohicans by James Fenimore Cooper

To Kill a Mockingbird by Harper Lee

The Joy Luck Club by Amy Tan

The Sun Also Rises by Ernest Hemingway

The Lord of the Flies by William Golding

Dangerous Minds by LouAnne Johnson

Schindler's List by Thomas Keneally

The Color of Water: A Black Man's Tribute to His White Mother by James McBride

On the Rez by Ian Frazier

The Bluest Eye by Toni Morrison

War

Red Badge of Courage by Stephen Crane
All Quiet on the Western Front by Erich Maria Remarque
Hiroshima by John Hershey
The Things They Carried by Tim O'Brien

Coming of Age

A Separate Peace by John Knowles
The Catcher in the Rye by J. D. Salinger
The House on Mango Street by Sandra Cisneros
The Adventures of Huckleberry Finn by Mark Twain
She's Come Undone by Wally Lamb

Short Stories

Try any short story collection by writers like Ernest Hemingway, Bobbie Ann Mason, Chinua Achebe, Isabel Allende, Flannery O'Connor, Joyce Carol Oates, O. Henry, Gabriel Garcia Marquez, Raymond Carver, Lorrie Moore, Nathan Englander, Ethan Canin, William Faulkner, Edgar Allen Poe, and others.

Inspirational/Spiritual

A Simple Path by Mother Theresa
The Tibetan Book of Living and Dying by Sogyal Rinpoche
Essays by Ralph Waldo Emerson
Care of the Soul by Thomas Moore
Chicken Soup for the Soul by Jack Canfield and Mark Victor Hansen
Hinds' Feet on High Places by Hannah Hurnard
The Tao of Pooh and *The Te of Piglet* by Benjamin Hoff
The Holy Bible
The Koran
Tao Te Ching by Lao Tzu
The Art of Happiness by the Dalai Lama and Howard C. Cutler

Detective/Thriller

Agatha Christie's murder mysteries
A Time To Kill, The Client by John Grisham
The *"A is for..."* series by Sue Grafton

Novels by Sara Paretsky
Sherlock Holmes stories by Sir Arthur Conan Doyle
Moonlight Becomes You and other novels by Mary Higgins Clark
Chromosome 6 and other books by Robin Cook

Increase Your Reading Speed

Below is a list of several books that can help you improve your reading speed.

- *21st Century Guide to Increasing Your Reading Speed* by Laurie E. Rozakis and Ellen Lichtenstein
- *Breakthrough Rapid Reading* by Peter Kump
- *How to Be a Rapid Reader: 6 Steps to Increased Speed and Concentration* by Kathryn Redway
- *Power Reading* by Laurie Rozakis
- *Power Reading: A Dynamic System for Mastering All Your Business Reading* by Phyllis Mindell
- *Rapid Reading in 5 Days: The Quick-And-Easy Program to Master Faster Reading* by Joan Minninger
- *Remember Everything You Read: The Evelyn Wood Seven-Day Speed Reading and Learning Program* by Stanley D. Frank
- *Speed Reading* by Tony Buzan
- *Super Reading Secrets* by Howard Stephen Berg
- *Triple Your Reading Speed* by Wade E. Cutler

APPENDIX B:
COMMON PREFIXES, SUFFIXES, AND WORD ROOTS

A familiarity with common prefixes, suffixes, and word roots can dramatically improve your ability to determine the meaning of unfamiliar vocabulary words. The tables below list common prefixes, suffixes, and word roots; their meanings; an example of a word with that prefix, suffix, or word root; the meaning of that word; and a sentence that demonstrates the meaning of that word. Refer to this appendix often to refresh your memory and improve your vocabulary.

PREFIXES
Prefixes are syllables added to the beginning of words to change or add to their meaning. This table lists some of the most common prefixes in the English language. They are listed in alphabetical order.

Prefix	Meaning	Example	Definition of Example	Sample Sentence
ante-	before	antevert (v)	to avert beforehand, prevent, anticipate	His decades of experience enabled him to **antevert** the problem.
anti-	against, opposite	antipode (n)	exact or direct opposite	North is the **antipode** of south.
auto-	by oneself or by itself	automaton (n)	a robot; a person who seems to act mechanically and without thinking	The workers on the assembly line looked like **automatons**.
bi-	two	bisect (v)	to divide into two equal parts	If you **bisect** a square, you will get two rectangles of equal size.
circum-	around	circumscribe (v)	to draw a line around; to mark the limits of	She carefully **circumscribed** the space that would become her office.
co-	together with; jointly	cohesive (adj)	having a tendency to bond or stick together; united	Though they came from different backgrounds and had many different interests, they have formed a remarkably **cohesive** team.
con-	with, together	consensus (n)	general agreement	After hours of debate, the group finally reached a **consensus** and selected a candidate.
contra-	against	contradict (v)	to state that (what is said) is untrue; to state the opposite of, be opposed to	I know we don't have to agree on everything, but she **contradicts** *everything* I say.
counter-	against, opposing	counterproductive (adj)	working against production	Complaining is **counterproductive**.
dis-	not, away, opposite of	dispel (v)	to drive away	To **dispel** rumors that I was quitting, I scheduled a series of meetings for the next three months.

Prefix	Meaning	Example	Definition of Example	Sample Sentence
duo-	two	duality (n)	having two sides or parts	The novel explores the **duality** of good and evil in humans.
ex-	out, from	expel (v)	to drive out or away	The rebels **expelled** the invaders.
in-	in, into	induct (v)	to bring in (to a group)	She was **inducted** into the honor society.
in-	not	invariable (adj)	not changing	The weather here is **invariable**—always sunny and warm.
inter-	between	intervene (v)	to come between	Romeo, trying to make peace, **intervened** in the fight between Tybalt and Mercutio.
inter-	together	interact (v)	to act upon or influence each other	The psychologist took notes as she watched the children **interact.**
intra-	within	intravenous (adj)	within or into a vein	She couldn't eat and had to be fed intra-**venously** for three days.
intro-	into, within	introvert (n)	a person whose attention is largely directed inward, toward himself or herself; a shy or withdrawn person	Unlike his flamboyant sister, quiet Zeke was a real **introvert.**
macro-	large	macrocosm (n)	the large scale world or universe; any great whole	Any change to the microcosm will eventually effect the **macrocosm.**
mal- ill	bad, wrong,	malaise (n)	feeling of discomfort or illness first few months of pregnancy is called "morning sickness."	The **malaise** many women feel during the
micro-	small	microcosm (n)	little or miniature world; something representing something else on a very small scale	Some people say that Brooklyn Heights, the Brooklyn district across the river from the Wall Street area, is a **microcosm** of Manhattan.

Prefix	Meaning	Example	Definition of Example	Sample Sentence
mini-	small	minority (n)	small group within a larger group	John voted for Bridget, but he was in the **minority**; most people voted for Elaine.
mis-	wrong, ill	misuse (v)	to use wrongly	She **misused** her authority when she reassigned Charlie to a new team.
mono-	one	monologue (n)	a long speech by one person or performer	I was very moved by the **monologue** in Scene III.
multi-	many	multifaceted (adj)	having many sides	This is a **multifaceted** issue, and we must examine each side carefully.
non-	not	nonviable (adj)	not able to live or survive	The doctor explained that the fetus was **nonviable**.
omni-	all	omniscient (adj)	knowing all	"God is **omniscient**," the preacher said. "There is nothing we can hide from Him."
pent-	five	pentameter (n)	a line of verse (poetry) with five metrical feet	Most of Shakespeare's sonnets are written in iambic **pentameter**.
poly-	many	polyglot (n)	one who speaks or understands several languages	It's no wonder he's a **polyglot**; he's lived in eight different countries.
post-	after	postscript (n)	message added after the close of a letter	His **postscript** was almost as long as his letter!
pre-	before	precede (v)	to come before in time or order	The appetizers **preceded** the main course.
pseudo-	false, fake	pseudonym (n)	false or fake name	Mark Twain is a **pseudonym** for Samuel Clemens.
quadr- quadri-	four	quadruped (n)	an animal with four feet	Some **quadrupeds** evolved into bipeds.

Prefix	Meaning	Example	Definition of Example	Sample Sentence
quint-	five	quintuplets (n)	five offspring born at one time	Each **quintuplet** weighed less than four pounds at birth.
sub-	under	subvert (v)	to bring about the destruction of, overthrow; to undermine	His attempt to **subvert** my authority will cost him his job.
super-	above, over	supervisor (n)	one who watches over	Alex refused the promotion to **supervisor** because he didn't feel comfortable being his friends' boss.
tetra-	four	tetralogy (n)	series of four related artistic works, such as plays, operas, novels, etc.	"Time Zone" was the fourth and final work in Classman's **tetralogy**.
tri-	three	triangle (n)	a figure having three angles	In an isosceles **triangle**, two of the three angles are the same size.
un-	not, against	unmindful (adj)	not conscious or aware of; forgetful	For better or worse, he is **unmindful** of office politics.
uni-	one	unify (v)	to form into a single unit, to unite	The new leader was able to **unite** the three factions into one strong political party.

SUFFIXES

Suffixes are syllables added to the ends of words to change or add to their meaning. This table lists some of the most common suffixes in the English language. They are listed in alphabetical order.

Suffix	Meaning	Example	Definition of Example	Sample Sentence
-acy	quality or state of	indeterminacy (n)	state or quality of being undetermined (without defined limits) or vague	The **indeterminacy** of his statement made it impossible to tell which side he was on.
-al	capable of, suitable for	practical (adj)	suitable for use; involving activity as distinct from study or theory	He has years of **practical**, on-the-job experience.
-ance -ence	quality or state of	tolerance (n)	willingness or ability to tolerate a person or thing	He has a high level of **tolerance** for rudeness.
-ary	place for, pertaining to	sanctuary (n)	a sacred place, refuge	With three noisy roommates, Ellen frequently sought the quiet **sanctuary** of the library.
-ate	to cause to be	resuscitate (v)	to bring or come back to life or consciousness; to revive	Thanks to a generous gift from an alumnus, we were able to **resuscitate** the study-abroad program.
-cide	kill	pesticide (n)	substance for killing insects	This **pesticide** is also dangerous for humans.
-en	to cause to become	broaden (v)	to make more broad, widen	Traveling around the world will **broaden** your understanding of other cultures.
-ful	full of	meaningful (adj)	significant, full of meaning	When Robert walked into the room with Annette, she cast me a **meaningful** glance.

Suffix	Meaning	Example	Definition of Example	Sample Sentence
-ial	pertaining to	commercial (adj)	of or engaged in commerce	**Commercial** vehicles must have special license plates.
-ic	pertaining to	aristocratic (adj)	of or pertaining to the aristocracy	Though he was never rich or powerful, he has very **aristocratic** manners.
-ify -fy	to make or cause to be	electrify (v)	to charge with electricity	The singer **electrified** the audience with her performance.
-ish	having the quality of	childish (adj)	like a child; unsuitable for a grown person	He didn't get the job because of his **childish** behavior during the interview.
-ism	quality, state, or condition of; doctrine of	optimism (n)	belief that things will turn out for the best; tendency to take a hopeful view of things	Her **optimism** makes people want to be around her.
-itis	inflammation of	tonsillitis (n)	inflammation and infection of the tonsils	Her **tonsillitis** was so severe that doctors had to remove her tonsils immediately.
-ity	quality or state of	morality (n)	state or quality of being moral	He argued that the basic **morality** of civilized societies hasn't changed much over the centuries.
-ive quality of	having the	descriptive (adj)	giving a description picture every place he had been.	The letter was so **descriptive** that I could
-ize	to make, to give	alphabetize (v)	to put in alphabetical order	Please **alphabetize** these files for me.
-less	lacking, free of	painless (adj)	without pain, not causing pain	The doctor assured me that it is a **painless** procedure.
-ly	resembling, having the qualities of	tenderly (adv)	done with tenderness; gently, delicately, lovingly	He held the newborn baby **tenderly** in his arms.

Suffix	Meaning	Example	Definition of Example	Sample Sentence
-ly	in the manner of	boldly (adv)	in a bold manner	Despite his fear, he stepped **boldly** onto the stage.
-ment	act or condition of	judgment (n)	ability to judge or make decisions wisely; act of judging	He exercised good **judgment** by keeping his mouth shut during the meeting.
-ology	the study of	zoology (n)	the scientific study of animal life	She took a summer job at the zoo even though it was unpaid because of her strong interest in **zoology**.
-or -er	one who does or performs the action of	narrator (n)	one who tells the story, gives an account of objective.	A first-person **narrator** is usually not
-ous -ose	full of	humorous (adj)	full of humor, funny	His **humorous** speech made the evening go by quickly.
-tion	act, state or condition of	completion (n)	the act of completing; the state of being	The second siren signaled completed or finished the **completion** of the fire drill.

COMMON LATIN WORD ROOTS

Many words in the English language have their origins in Latin. The table below shows several original Latin words that we have used to create various English words. The Latin words serve as **roots**, providing the core meaning of the words; prefixes, suffixes, and other alterations give each word its distinct meaning. The word roots are listed in alphabetical order.

Root	Meaning	Example	Definition of Example	Sample Sentence
amare	to love	amorous (adj)	readily showing or feeling love	She told him to stop his **amorous** advances as she was already engaged.
audire	to hear	audience (n)	assembled group of listeners or spectators; people within hearing	The **audience** was stunned when the game show host slapped the contestant.
capere	to take	captivate (v)	to capture the fancy of	The story **captivated** me from the beginning; I couldn't put the book down.
dicere	to say, speak	dictate (v)	to state or order; to say what needs to be written down	She began to **dictate** her notes into the microphone.
duco	to lead	conduct (v)	to lead or guide	He **conducted** a detailed tour of the building.
equus	equal	equilibrium (n)	a state of balance	I have finally achieved an **equilibrium** between work and leisure.
facere	to make or do	manufacture (v)	to make or produce	The clothes are **manufactured** here in this factory.
lucere	to light	lucid (adj)	very clear	No one could possibly have misunderstood such a **lucid** explanation.
manus	hand	manicure (n)	cosmetic treatment of the fingernails	To take care of her long fingernails, she gets a **manicure** every week.

Root	Meaning	Example	Definition of Example	Sample Sentence
medius	middle	median (n)	middle point; middle in a set of numbers	The **median** household income in this wealthy neighborhood is $89,000.
mittere	to send	transmit (v)	to send across	The message was **transmitted** over the intercom.
omnis	all, every	omnipresent (adj)	present everywhere	That top-40 song is **omnipresent**; everywhere I go, I hear it playing.
plicare	to fold	application (n)	putting one thing on another; making a formal request	His loan **application** was denied because of his poor credit history.
ponere positum	to place	position (n)	the place a person or thing occupies	Although he is only 22, he holds a very powerful **position** in the company.
protare	to carry	transport (v)	to carry across	The goods will be **transported** by boat.
quarere	to ask, question	inquiry (n)	act of inquiry, investigation, or questioning	The **inquiry** lasted several months but yielded no new information.
scribere	to write	scribe (n)	person who makes copies of writings	The **scribe** had developed thick calluses on his fingers from years of writing.
sentire	to feel	sentient (adj)	capable of feeling	No **sentient** beings should be used for medical research.
specere	to look at	spectacle (n)	striking or impressive sight	The debate was quite a **spectacle**—you should've seen the candidates attack one another.
spirare	to breathe	respiration (n)	the act of breathing	His **respiration** was steady, but he remained unconscious.

Root	Meaning	Example	Definition of Example	Sample Sentence
tendere	to stretch	extend (v)	to make longer, stretch out	Please **extend** the deadline by two weeks, so we can complete the project properly.
verbum	word	verbatim (adj)	word for word	The student failed because she had copied an article **verbatim** instead of writing her own essay.

COMMON GREEK WORD ROOTS

Many other English words have their origins in the ancient Greek language. The table below shows several Greek words that we have used to create various English words. The Greek words serve as **roots,** providing the core meaning of the words; prefixes, suffixes, and other alterations give each word its distinct meaning. The word roots are listed in alphabetical order.

Root	Meaning	Example	Definition of Example	Sample Sentence
bios	life	biology (n)	the science of living organisms	He is majoring in **biology** and plans to go to medical school.
chronos	time	chronological (adj)	arranged in the order in which things occurred	The story is confusing because she did not put the events in **chronological** order.
derma	skin	dermatology (n)	branch of medical science dealing with the skin and its diseases	She has decided to study **dermatology** because she has always been plagued by rashes.
gamos	marriage, union	polygamy (n)	the practice or custom of having more than one spouse or mate at a time	The Mormons are one of the few religious groups that practice **polygamy**.
genos	race, sex, kind	genocide (n)	deliberate extermination of one race of people	The recent **genocide** in Bosnia has created a crisis in orphaned children.
geo	earth	geography (n)	the study of the Earth's surface; the surface or topographical features of a place	The **geography** of this region made it difficult for the different tribes to interact.
graphein	to write	calligraphy (n)	beautiful or elegant handwriting	She used **calligraphy** when she addressed the wedding invitations.
krates	member of a group	democrat (n) as a principle of government	one who believes in or advocates democracy	I have always been a **democrat**, but I refuse to join the Democratic Party.
kryptos	hidden, secret	cryptic (adj)	concealing meaning, puzzling	He left such a **cryptic** message on my answering machine that I don't know what he wanted.

Root	Meaning	Example	Definition of Example	Sample Sentence
metron	to measure	metronome (n)	device with a pendulum that beats at a determined rate to measure time/rhythm	She used a **metronome** to help her keep the proper pace as she played the song.
morphe	form	polymorphous (adj)	having many forms	Most mythologies have a **polymorphous** figure, a "shape shifter" who can be both animal and human.
pathos	suffering, feeling	pathetic (adj)	arousing feelings of pity or sadness	Willy Loman is a complex character who is both **pathetic** and heroic.
philos	loving	xenophile (n)	a person who is attracted to foreign people, cultures, or customs	Alex is a **xenophile**; I doubt he'll ever come back to America.
phobos	fear	xenophobe (n)	person who fears or hates foreigners or strange cultures or customs	Don't expect Len to go on the trip; he's a **xenophobe.**
photos	light	photobiotic (adj)	living or thriving only in the presence of light	Plants are **photobiotic** and will die without light.
podos	foot	podiatrist (n)	an expert in diagnosis and treatment of ailments of the human foot	The **podiatrist** saw that the ingrown toenail had become infected.
pyr	fire	pyromaniac (n)	one who has a compulsion to set things on fire	The warehouse fire was not an accident; it was set by a **pyromaniac.**
soma	body	psychosomatic (adj)	of or involving both the mind and body	In a **psychosomatic** illness, physical symptoms are caused by emotional distress.
tele	distant	telescope (n)	optical instrument for making distant objects appear larger and nearer when viewed through the lens	While Galileo did not invent the **telescope**, he was the first to use it to study the planets and stars.
therme	heat	thermos (n)	insulated jug or bottle that keeps liquids hot or ~~cold~~	The **thermos** kept my coffee hot all afternoon.

INDEX

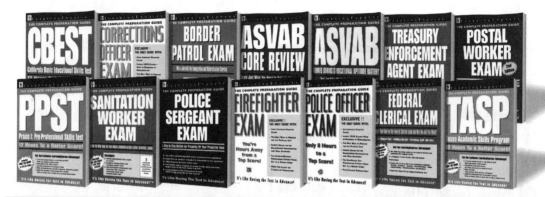